Space and Ocean Exploration

Space and Ocean Exploration

THE ALTERNATIVE TO THE MILITARY
INDUSTRIAL COMPLEX

Danny Quintana

ISBN: 1517056802
ISBN 13: 9781517056803

Acknowledgements

I had the good fortune to have Dr. Francis D. Wormuth as my mentor. He was a genius of the first order, a critical thinker and an intellectual. Thanks to the Rockefeller Foundation for helping me while I was a poor, struggling college student. The true measure of wealth is what good you do in the world. The Rockefeller family has done much good for mankind with responsible use of their assets. Thanks to my son Isaac Quintana, his wife Natalie, my partner Bridgette Martin Turner, Aaron Crabtree and Mark Quayle my financial analyst and friend. Thanks to Lois Collins, a lifelong friend who keeps me focused. I give special thanks to Jesus and his message of love, charity and forgiveness. If we practice this message, our lives and the world will be as one. The proceeds of this book are used to help our Quintana Family Trust deliver wheelchairs to the disabled in the developing world.

Dedication

To my mentor Dr. Francis D. Wormuth and my grandmother Ramonsita Quintana. Thank you for your wisdom, knowledge and guidance.

Preface

> War is peace.
> — GEORGE ORWELL

This book is a practical policy alternative to reduce defense spending without increasing unemployment. It is common knowledge the United States spends more money on defense than the next 20 nations **combined.** Clearly, much of the spending is hidden from public scrutiny in other agencies and re-labeled under other priorities. The true size of the United States defense budget was approximately $931 billion for 2013. This spending is justified to fight a new enemy, "terrorists". The "War on Terror" replaced the previous enemy, "Godless Communism," which replaced the previous enemy, "fascism".

Although it is no longer true, many people on our small planet believe the United States is the greatest threat to world peace. Since World War II, the United States has bombed more nations, supported more dictators and invaded more countries than all other nations **combined.** From 1945 to 2015, the United States dropped more bombs on other nations than all ordnance used in World War I and II. Over 3,000,000 people have been killed by American-created conflicts and millions more have been wounded. Entire nations have been destroyed and millions of refugees have been created. We remain the most powerful nation in humanity's history. Endless war has not brought peace.

All 435 U.S. congressional districts have either a defense contractor or a military installation. As of 2015, the United States has 730 military installations in 50 countries. The Department of Defense is the nation's largest employer. Defense industries are so intertwined with the economy that the United States can't just "cut" defense spending. That would create unemployment in thousands of communities. That is why we need an economically viable alternative to defense spending.

Eisenhower's "Military Industrial Complex" is actually a giant economic program created by the defense spending coalition. This coalition includes universities, labor unions, agricultural communities, the various branches of the military and, obviously, defense contractors and their allies in Congress. It is one of the most powerful lobbies in Congress. The defense spending coalition will get the tax dollars, so it seems prudent to give them a new mission.

I propose Congress redirect some of this defense spending toward space and ocean exploration. This will demilitarize the American economy and create millions of new jobs as well as entire new industries. Give the aerospace contractors exploration of the inner solar system. They are naturally suited to transition from "defense" to space exploration. Mars needs to be explored, terraformed and colonized. It is doable in our lifetime and, if civilization is to survive, it must be pursued.

Because of the costly failure of the Iraq War, we can no longer pursue space exploration alone. We will need to work with the Chinese, Russians, the European Union, India and Brazil as well as other countries to pull off this massive endeavor. The Iraq war broke the bank. Space and ocean exploration can fix our economic problems. Using the aerospace and navy contractors and congressional districts, explore the inner solar system and the ocean floor.

The only area on this small planet that has not been fully explored is the ocean floor. If U.S. Navy contractors can build nuclear submarines, they can build ocean-mining vessels and robots to explore the ocean bottom. Trust me, the ocean bottom is at least as interesting as the moon's behind.

The fish stocks are collapsing. We propose the creation of a Global High Seas Marine Preserve, closing off the high seas to commercial fishing. The U.S. Navy working with navies of other countries can enforce wildlife zones in the oceans that will revive the fish stocks. The problem of the collapse of the fish stocks and plastic in the ocean cannot be solved with 10 U.S. aircraft carrier battle groups or by one nation. We need to work together with other nations. Ecosystems do not recognize national boundaries.

The Iraq war was an expensive moral disaster. Approximately 1 million Iraqis have been killed, millions more are wounded and over 4 million are refugees. Iraq is now engaged in a proxy war between Iran and Saudi Arabia. The actual cost of the war was over $3 trillion dollars and paid for on credit. The civil war between the Shia and the Sunni continues and has spilled over to neighboring countries. Needless to say, not one drop of oil was created by this war. It did nothing to improve "national security." In fact, it made the world less secure.

Despite the huge environmental problems facing our tiny planet, I am optimistic. Environmental problems can be solved. With governments, industry and non-profits all working together, we can and will change humanity's path from consumerism and conspicuous consumption to sustainability and co-existence with our Earth Mother. Young people understand environmental problems and are willing to make a difference. Be optimistic — the change begins with you.

Table of Contents

"To look at the sky, and behold the wondrous heart of silence. I have thought, and studied, and worked for years, and I know so little — all I can do is to adore when I behold this unfailing regularity, the miraculous balance and perfect adaptation. The majesty of it all humbles me to dust."

— COPERNICUS

PART I

Why We Fight
Our Economic Model and
American Imperialism

CHAPTER 1

Journey Through
The War Factory

> "You shall not be like the hypocrites. For
> they love to pray standing in the synagogues
> and on the corners of the streets."
> — MATTHEW 6:5

Why should we redirect taxpayer money from defense to space and ocean exploration? Why explore the cosmos and the oceans?

The answer is found in human history. When humans came out of Africa we explored, competed for empire and colonized. We conquered the land areas of our planet. The fact that we still have militaries is indicative of our prior conquests. The United States has 1.4 million men and women under arms.[1] While the number seems quite large, we have to remember there are over 310 million people living in the lower 48 states. Globally, there are approximately 40 million people under arms[2]. With a human population of approximately 7.2 billion, that is not a large number.

In the United States, our military is in the shadows, on bases at home and overseas. Our military is not hostile to the public. We know these troops. They are family members and friends. Some of us work at defense installations or for the various defense contractors.

The current economic model of consumer spending is supported by the world's largest defense budget. This model can and must change for obvious reasons. The United States is the greatest military power in human history. Our country has ten aircraft carrier battle groups and 730 military installations in 50 countries.[3] With less than 5 percent of the planet's population, we consume approximately 20 percent of the world's oil; produce more than 40 percent of the carbon dioxide that affects climate change and create more municipal solid waste garbage per capita than any other nation.[4]

US military bases world wide 2001-2003

In this period the United States has over 730 military installations and bases in over 50 countries.
It also has military personnel on active duty in dozens of other countries.

We created this consumption economy with empire. After World War II ended, the United States stepped into the shoes of the collapsed British Empire and inherited an imperial role in world affairs. Americans preached democracy at home, yet supported brutal dictators and strong men around the planet. This was a disaster for millions of people and for global economic development.

The model that was created was a massive military-industrial complex, a popular term coined by President Dwight D. Eisenhower in his now-famous farewell address. It should more appropriately be called the military-industrial-labor unions-universities coalition — in short, the defense spending coalition. This growth in defense spending has occurred for the same reasons any other quest for more money and power takes place in society. It is the normal push of bureaucratic inertia and the natural growth of organizations. Whether it is the Drug Enforcement Agency, Health and Human Services, the Social Security Administration or any other government agency or corporate organization, growth is a natural process. With this growth comes power from the broad-based number of individuals that have a vested interested in money being spent on this sector. Bureaucratic growth is a natural phenomenon that results in political spending cycles that feed on themselves.

With political roots that trace to the Civil War and military installations or industries in every congressional district, the military-industrial complex is the embodiment of political power in America. A journey through the American war factory illustrates the reach and strength of the defense spending coalition. Only by understanding the depth and scale of the defense spending coalition and vast infrastructure can we come up with an alternative.

We cannot just "cut defense spending." Without an economic alternative, the result would be unemployment in the communities where defense spending provides a livelihood. It does not matter where you live in America, within one hour from your home in every major city of every state there is either a defense contractor or a military base. This need for employment created the National Security State permanent war so the post-World War II economy would not collapse like it did during the Great Depression. Hitler and Tojo lifted the U.S. economy out of the Great Depression.

Defense spending took off because policy planners were terrified of another economic collapse; consequently, the arms race became economic policy. Planners mistakenly believed war was good for the economy. Defense spending is economic policy, albeit a poor alternative to more productive expenditures.

After World War II, numerous rural agricultural communities lost their young to the jobs, excitement and entertainment possibilities of urban America. They had to find work somewhere and the defense industries provided employment. Consequently, thousands of communities nationwide depend on defense spending to provide jobs.

Since all 435 congressional districts have a defense contractor and/or a military installation, there is little incentive to oppose self-serving spending that will create very few jobs. With more than 5,000 bases of all types in the United States as of 2015, every area of the country is affected by the defense budget. Increasing defense spending is popular with Congress.[5]

Both political parties voted for the Iraq war. The United States, in violation of international law, invaded Iraq, a country that had nothing to do with 9/11. This was a historic event that brought about the end of Pax Americana.

Conflicts in this century will be battles over ideas and economics. Military conflicts between nation-states with huge land armies like those of the last century's two world wars are obsolete. The United States cannot attack Brazil, China, Russia or any large country in a ground war. But nations can engage in major trade, sporting events, international art exhibits and together explore the inner solar system.

The Iraq war changed human history. Now the United States is one nation on a planet with many nations. We are not "special" or "a shining city on a hill" or "the greatest nation on Earth." Other citizens love their countries, too. Yet despite our flaws, the world is a better place because of the United States' military. Working together with other nations, all human-created global problems can be solved. We can have the collective security that was envisioned by the founders of the United Nations. This can only happen with a new economic model not based upon defense spending and consumerism. As Admiral Eugene Carroll observed:

> "For 45 years of the Cold War we were in an arms race with the Soviet Union. Now it appears we're in an arms race with ourselves." *Admiral Eugene Carroll, Jr., U.S. Navy (Ret.) Deputy Director Center for Defense Information*[6]

---

1 "United States Armed Forces,."Wikipedia. Accessed July 22, 2015. http://en.wikipedia.org/wiki/United_States_Armed_Forces.
2 "List of Countries by Number of Military and Paramilitary Personnel." Wikipedia. Accessed July 22, 2015. http://en.wikipedia.org/wiki/List_of_countries_by_number_of_military_and_paramilitary_personnel.
3 "USA Empire Has 730 Military Bases in 50 Countries." http://www.dailykos.com/story/2007/06/18/347765/-USA-Empire-has-730-Military-bases-in-50-countries#. and United States Navy website at: "Navy.mil Home Page."The US Navy. Accessed July 22, 2015. http://www.navy.mil/navydata/fact_display.asp?cid=4200&tid=200&ct=4.

4 "Use It and Lose It: The Outsize Effect of U.S. Consumption on the Environment." Scientific American Global RSS. Accessed July 22, 2015. http://www.scientificamerican.com/article/american-consumption-habits/.

5 Our Global Infrastructure "The national security depends on our defense installations and facilities being in the right place, at the right time, with the right qualities and capacities to protect our national resources. Those resources have never been more important as America fights terrorists who plan and carry out attacks on our facilities and our people. Our military service members and civilians operate in every time zone and in every climate. More than 450,000 employees are overseas, both afloat and ashore. The Defense Department manages an inventory of installations and facilities to keep Americans safe. The Department's physical plant is huge by any standard, consisting of more than several hundred thousand individual buildings and structures located at more than 5,000 different locations or sites. When all sites are added together, the Department of Defense utilizes over 30 million acres of land. These sites range from the very small in size such as unoccupied sites supporting a single navigational aid that sit on less than one-half acre, to the Army's vast White Sands Missile Range in New Mexico with over 3.6 million acres, or the Navy's large complex of installations at Norfolk, Virginia with more than 78,000 employees. In Comparison, in terms of people and operations, we're busier than just about all of the nation's largest private sector companies.

The Department of Defense has a budget of four $419.3 dollars and more than three million employees; Wal-Mart has a budget of about $227 billion and employs about one-point-three million people; Department of Defense online at: "United States Department of Defense." About The Department of Defense. Accessed July 22, 2015. http://www.defense.gov/about/dod101.aspx.

6 "A Cold War Budget Without a Cold War?, Page 1." AboveTopSecret.com. Accessed July 22, 2015. http://www.abovetopsecret.com/forum/thread208793/pg1.

CHAPTER 2

Don't Blame the Military for the Military-Industrial Complex

> "Worse than traitors in arms are the
> men who pretend loyalty to the flag,
> feast and fatten on the misfortunes
> of the nation while patriotic blood is
> crimsoning the plains of the south and their
> countrymen are moldering in the dust."
> — ABRAHAM LINCOLN

The excesses in defense spending and consumerism cannot be blamed on our men and women in uniform who try so hard to guard our freedoms and protect our liberties. We are in a century with unusual enemies and a different mission for our armed forces. We no longer face totalitarian empires like the former Soviet Union or Nazi Germany. Warfare today is asymmetrical. Lone wolves and small criminal organizations using the pretext of religion are the danger to global peace. Whether it is the international narcotics trade or religious terrorism, large armies are not what the world is fighting. We have an international crime problem, not a conflict with fascism or communism. We are fighting suicide bombers and international drug dealers, not well-armed soldiers with uniforms, planes, tanks and heavy battleships. Intelligence and detective work, not aircraft carrier battle groups, will win the day.

Large nation states, like India, China, Pakistan and Brazil have their hands full just managing their large populations. These countries have major economic ties to the West. The Chinese are interested in developing their economy and internal stability, not in ruling the world. With a population of over 1.3 billion, the Chinese government has massive internal political, economic and environmental problems.[1]

In the last century, our politicians often used our military as the enforcer for big business. As Major General Smedley Butler, U.S. Marine Corps., observed in 1933:

"War is just a racket. A racket is best described, I believe, as something that is not what it seems to the majority of people. Only a small inside group knows what it is about. It is conducted for the benefit of the very few at the expense of the masses.

I believe in adequate defense at the coastline and nothing else. If a nation comes over here to fight, then we'll fight. The trouble with America is that when the dollar only earns 6 percent over here, then it gets restless and goes overseas to get 100 percent. Then the flag follows the dollar and the soldiers follow the flag.

I wouldn't go to war again as I have done to protect some lousy investment of the bankers. There are only two things we should fight for. One is the defense of our homes and the other is the Bill of Rights. War for any other reason is simply a racket.

There isn't a trick in the racketeering bag that the military gang is blind to. It has its "finger men" to point out enemies, its "muscle men" to destroy enemies, its "brain men" to plan war preparations, and a "Big Boss," Super-Nationalistic-Capitalism. Looking back on it, I feel that I could have given Al Capone a few hints. The best he could do was to operate his racket in three districts. I operated on three continents." [2]

In a world where major multinational corporations transcend the legal reach of any nation state, the American military machine no longer has the role of protecting the free world from the dangers of global communism. Far greater dangers come from international viruses like AIDS, Ebola and from economic dislocation from globalization. Both are here to stay and will not be eradicated or controlled any time soon.

The military does not set public policy. They are asked to do the unpleasant task of carrying out political objectives, regardless of how ill-advised. If that means the angry jungles of Vietnam or the hot deserts of Iraq or the mountains of Afghanistan, then our military is there and ready. It also means the troops are stuck with weapon systems they don't want, programs they don't need and military hardware that is not appropriate for today's challenges. The history of weapons procurement in Washington is one of intrigue, duplicity and pork barrel politics. [3]

If a credible threat does not exist, then lie to justify the spending. In the words of the infamous Hermann Goring

(1945): "The people can always be brought to the bidding of the leaders. All you have to do is tell them they are being attacked and then denounce the peacemakers for lack of patriotism." [4]

Politics was the decisive factor in going forward with major defense programs, from the B-70 bomber to the B-1, the B-2, various nuclear submarines, the Nimitz aircraft carriers, the MX weapons system, the Osprey helicopter to the missile defense system and the F-22 fighter and F-35 fighter program.. [5]

With subcontractors in numerous congressional districts, these weapon programs have popular appeal. The funding by Congress of the various weapon systems meant major financial gain as each system costs millions of dollars per product. The B-1 cost over $200 million per plane without armaments or support bases. [6] These planes provided handsome profits for Rockwell International, the builder, and General Electric, one of the world's largest corporations, which provided the engine. [7]

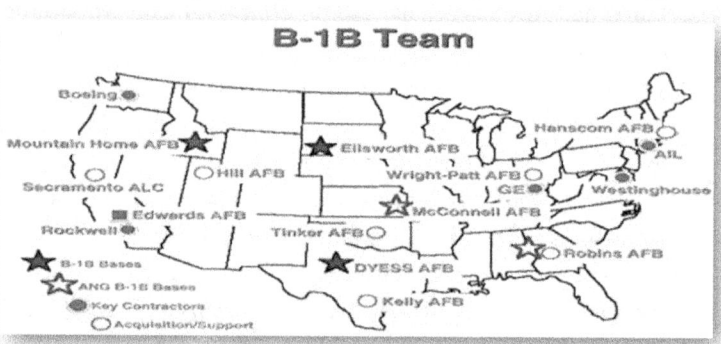

Northrop Grumman did well as the prime contractor of this expensive plane. The subcontractors were spread out throughout the nation to force the program down the public's and the military's throat. These bombers succeeded politically as well as technologically. The B-2 bomber was a political pork barrel project, not a military necessity. In the end, the bomber was found not to be as effective as far less expensive alternatives.[7]

These impressive weapons systems are the wrong solution for the challenges of this century. Major weapons systems were absolutely necessary for the last century when America was fighting the Nazis, Japanese imperialism in Asia and competing with the Soviet Union. They do not work against religious extremists who are determined to kill others even if they have to kill themselves in the process. Today's suicide bombers, international drug dealers and lone wolf killers cannot be stopped by nuclear submarines, expensive fighter planes or aircraft carrier battle groups.

A $12 billion dollar aircraft carrier will do wonders for the defense contractors who build this massive weapons system. It will not make the nation or the world safer from criminals. Much of the defense budget has more to do with the projection of American power and protection of American interests. The military is left out of the policy equation and is too often saddled with weapons systems and bases that are not necessary for the mission at hand. Politics, not military necessity, will continue to fuel defense spending.

Congress will refuse to close military bases in politically powerful districts despite the Pentagon wanting to shut them down. Congress will allocate more fighter planes then the Air Force needs. Congress, not the military and not the Executive branch, has control of the purse strings. This political reality existed prior to September 11, 2001, and continues today.

But simple things like suggesting an increase in military pay create a firestorm of controversy. There are lobbyists for fighter planes, ships and artillery pieces. But paying a competitive salary to our soldiers to stay in the military is not always a high priority with Congress. Like schoolteachers, we expect a lot from them but are unwilling to properly pay for their services. The people who protect this country are willing to give their lives to insure we have a Bill of Rights and that our homes and streets are safe. They do not keep the profits that come from major weapons systems and they do not get votes for their re-election.

Despite the criticism of these expensive weapon systems being inappropriate in the days of suicide bombers and snipers, the defense industry pushes forward. With allies in Congress they continue to make a mockery of the defense needs of this country and the free world. Our young men and women in the military love our country and do wonderful work all over the world.

Our military is a global force for good, from providing aid to the victims of the devastating tsunami that killed hundreds of thousands of people in Thailand and Indonesia to protecting school children in Iraq. Our men and women who serve this nation should be paid and paid well. Our defense contractors are well paid. Let's pay the people who are actually protecting us more money. They are worth it.

---

1 Several sources online describe in detail China's challenging internal political and economic problems. While dated, this article is still very relevant. Haass, Richard N. "China's Greatest Threat Is Internal." Council on Foreign Relations. December 28, 2011. Accessed July 23, 2015. http://www.cfr.org/china/chinas-greatest-threat-internal/p26930.

2 Butler, Smedley D., General. "War Is a Racket." Wikipedia. Accessed July 23, 2015. http://en.wikipedia.org/wiki/War_Is_a_Racket.

3 Sweigart, Josh. "Congress Pushes for Weapons Pentagon Didn't Want." Congress Pushes for Weapons Pentagon Didn't Want. August 20, 2012. Accessed July 23, 2015. http%3A%2F%2Fwww.military.com%2Fdaily-

news%2F2012%2F08%2F20%2Fcongress-pushes-for-weapons-pentagon-didnt-want.html.

4 Hermann Goering, "Why, of course the people don't want war. Why should some poor slob on a farm want to risk his life in a war when the best he can get out of it is to come back to his farm in one piece? Naturally the common people don't want war: neither in Russia, nor in England, nor for that matter in Germany. That is understood. But after all, it is the leaders of a country who determine the policy and it is always a simple matter to drag the people along, whether it is a democracy or fascist dictatorship, or a parliament or a communist dictatorship. Voice or no voice, the people can always be brought to the bidding of the leaders. That is easy. All you have to do is tell them they are being attacked, and denounce the peacemakers for lack of patriotism and exposing the country to danger. It works the same in any country." Goering, Hermann. "A Quote by Hermann Goering." Goodreads. Accessed July 23, 2015. https://www.goodreads.com/quotes/33505-why-of-course-the-people-don-t-want-war-why-should.

5 Hollaran, Richard. "Reagan Moving on Start of Fleet of New Bombers." February 22, 1981. http%3A%2F%2Fwww.nytimes.com%2F1981%2F02%2F22%2Fus%2Freagan-moving-on-start-of-fleet-of-new-bombers.html. See, Rockwell B-1 Lancer with a unit cost of over $280 million per plane and stationed in several states; this expensive bomber illustrates how politics will win out over alternatives. Online at: "B-1 Lancer." Wikipedia. Accessed July 23, 2015. https://en.wikipedia.org/wiki/Rockwell_B-1_Lancer. The Northrop Grumman B-2 Spirit has a unit cost of over $730 million dollars per plane. The 21 planes are still operational and stationed at various base throughout the United States and at times overseas. Online at: "Northrop Grumman B-2 Spirit." Wikipedia. Accessed July 23, 2015. https://en.wikipedia.org/wiki/Northrop_Grumman_B-2_Spirit. *Virginia*-class submarine has a unit cost of approximately $2.6 billion. Online at: "Virginia-class Submarine." Wikipedia. Accessed July 23, 2015. https://en.wikipedia.org/wiki/Virginia-class_submarine. Bell Boeing V-22 Osprey is a $36 billion program and has a unit cost of over $72 million. Online at: Bell Boeing V-22 Osprey. https://en.wikipedia.org/wiki/Bell_Boeing_V-22_Osprey. United States national missile defense. The costs of deploying a effective missile defense system is unknown and has come

under extensive criticism. Counter-measures can be taken, such as driving a truck under the system or parking a trawler in the harbor of an enemy state. See "United States National Missile Defense." https://en.wikipedia.org/wiki/United_States_national_missile_defense. The Lockheed Martin F-22 Raptor is the most advanced fighter plane ever built. With a unit cost of over $150 million this fighter will rule the skies for the foreseeable future. See "Lockheed Martin F-22 Raptor." Wikipedia. Accessed July 23, 2015. http://en.wikipedia.org/wiki/Lockheed_Martin_F-22_Raptor. 6.- 8. Ibid, cites supra

CHAPTER 3

A New Role for the World's Militaries

> "The Indians are so naïve and free with
> their possessions that no one who has not
> witnessed them would believe it. When you
> ask them for something they have, they never
> say no. To the contrary, they offer to share
> with anyone. They would make fine servants.
> With fifty men we could subjugate them
> all and make them do whatever we want."
> — CHRISTOPHER COLUMBUS

One of the most amazing advances in human history has been our increasing knowledge of the vastness of the universe. In the short span of 500 years, the travel time on our planet has greatly diminished. Today, flights to the other side of the world are routine. In the mere span of 18 hours, humans can fly from Salt Lake City, Utah, U.S.A., to Sydney, Australia. Most of the world's major cities are connected by 22 hours of flight time. Our small planet is interconnected by the Internet, jet travel, international trade, telecommunications satellites and common laws that govern all of us who are civilized. The International Standards Organization sets over 20,000 standards for manufacturing on a whole host of industries. This furthers international trade.[1] There are numerous international conventions on the environment, trade and crime. Law exists.

Our ancestors had a much larger planet. You usually only went on the 1,600 mile Camino Real de Tierra Adentro from Mexico City to Santa Fe one time. The trip was six months long and dangerous.[2] Travel was on horseback or foot with numerous stops. If you survived on the 2,000 mile Oregon Trail and made it to the rich lands of the northwest you did not go back. The trek would take four to five months.[3] In addition to being subjected to the elements, the various Indian tribes who were fighting to preserve their way of life might attack you. Accidents were common. Crime was another danger. A wrong turn might mean death from starvation or thirst. The journey was not for the faint of heart.

Today, the drive from Salt Lake City, Utah, to Portland, Oregon, is 13 hours driving in air-conditioned vehicles complete with music and comfortable seats on well-maintained roads. There are numerous rest stops, nice hotels, restaurants and sightseeing along the way. If you choose to fly, the trip is about two hours. National and global tourism are huge multibillion dollar industries. All of this is possible because the planet's militaries keep the peace.

Obviously, the criminals of our small planet do not feel bound by the rule of law and will rob travelers, blow up restaurants and schools, kidnap, rob, steal, sell dangerous illegal drugs and do what ill-mannered scum throughout history have done: crime. Here, the world's militaries work to keep the peace. The fact that humans can travel from the United States to places our ancestors would only dream about is itself a remarkable testimony of how much progress we have made in a mere 500 years. Law, technology and the world's militaries enable humans to visit Beijing, Moscow, Bali, Paris, Puerto Vallarta, Vancouver British Columbia, Machu Picchu, the wildlife safaris of Kenya, islands in the Caribbean or just the beautiful national parks here in the United States. The world's militaries work as global police forces to keep the peace, protect trade and travelers and enforce international laws.

Because of our advancement in space research and exploration, we are now aware of other dangers. Asteroids could take out the entire planet and there is the probability of alien civilizations in other parts of our huge galaxy. In this century, the global militaries will be required to engage in mankind's most important missions. In addition to protecting the planet from criminals, in this century global militaries need to protect the planet from asteroids and develop super weapons.

Scientists are reaching out to the universe, trying to contact other life forms. This is a big mistake. We should continue to discover what is out there. But contacting civilizations far more advanced than humans who are still fighting over pieces of land based upon religious books written thousands of years ago is not prudent. WHEN we encounter other life forms, they are going to be hostile, far more advanced and extremely dangerous. The physicist Stephen Hawkins holds the chair at Oxford once held by Sir Isaac Newton. He had this to say about alien life forms:

"To my mathematical brain, the numbers alone make thinking about aliens perfectly rational," he said, according to The Sunday Times. "The real challenge is working out what aliens might actually be like."

Hawking says that they could be microbes – basic animals such as worms which have been on Earth for millions of years, but suggests that extraterrestrial life could develop much further. "We only have to look at ourselves to see how intelligent life might develop into something we wouldn't want to meet," Hawking said. "I imagine they might exist in massive ships, having used up all the resources from their home planet. Such advanced aliens would perhaps become nomads, looking to conquer and colonize whatever planets they can reach."

The scientist, who is paralyzed by motor neuron disease, warned that contact with alien life could spell disaster for the human race. "If aliens ever visit us, I think the outcome would be much as when Christopher Columbus first landed in America, which didn't turn out very well for the American Indians." [3]

The worlds' scientists need to work together on space-based weapons for the not-so-distant threats of asteroids hitting the planet. We don't know how much time we have before we encounter other alien civilizations. Time goes by very fast. The dangers we face might be decades away or just a few years. Our efforts to contact other civilizations might have been successful. Thus humans have to work together to face common threats.

Asteroids have been slamming into the earth since the planet was formed. The most common theory on the extinction of the dinosaurs is an asteroid hit the earth. The impact was so great the dust and debris blocked out the sun, altered the weather and known life on the planet ended. Humans await the same fate. But unlike the dinosaurs, we have opposable thumbs and technology. Here is what some scientists speculate would happen if a giant asteroid hit the earth:

> By the time you get up to a mile-wide asteroid, you are working in the 1 million megaton range. This aster-oid has the energy that's 10 million times greater than the bomb that fell on Hiroshima. It's able to flatten

everything for 100 to 200 miles out from ground zero. In other words, if a mile-wide asteroid were to directly hit New York City, the force of the impact probably would completely flatten every single thing from Washington D.C. to Boston, and would cause extensive damage perhaps 1,000 miles out — that's as far away as Chicago. The amount of dust and debris thrown up into the atmosphere would block out the sun and cause most living things on the planet to perish. If an asteroid that big were to land in the ocean, it would cause massive tidal waves hundreds of feet high that would completely scrub the coastlines in the vicinity.[4]

The United States trades with the world. The Chinese, Japanese, Arabs and Europeans buy American bonds. A land war with China, Russia, Germany, Japan, Mexico or any other country is highly unlikely in this century. History has just moved on from the days of Hitler, Stalin and Mao. Clearly the threats from criminal elements that hide behind religion will continue for the foreseeable future. These little religious hoodlums who blow up mosques and schools and shoot girls in the face for wanting an education will not go away in our lifetime. They will continue to cause a lot of human suffering. Religious hoodlums and international drug dealers are not an existential threat to the survival of the species and all life on this planet. They just need to be prosecuted and if convicted of the numerous crimes they are committing, jailed.

In a world where we are a mere 22 hours apart, like each other or not, the threats from an asteroid hitting the earth is common to all governments. Contacting alien life forms that can come to our tiny planet and devour us is a common danger.

Battling super viruses that could kill life on this planet is a common threat. Fighting the criminals require the militaries of the planet to work together. Fortunately for humans, we already have the necessary military might to keep the peace. We do not have the military to protect our tiny planet from asteroids or unwelcome invaders. We need to develop a global military for a space-based planetary defense primarily to protect the planet from asteroids, not space aliens. It is a question of when, not if our planet will be hit by asteroids. Contact by civilizations far more advanced than our own is possible, the planet being destroyed by an asteroid is probable. The math is there.

Life in other parts of the universe is probably. We now know there are billions of planets in the Goldilocks zone. These are planets that are close enough to a star to support life but not so far that it is too cold; it is just the right distance.[5] There are billions of galaxies and hundreds of billions of planets capable of having life. The mathematical probability that there are other life forms out there in a universe with billions of stars and billions of planets means humans and dolphins here on this tiny planet are not alone in the universe.

Fortunately we are at great distances from even the nearest star. Asteroids are a different story. To be so imprudent and arrogant as to not prepare for an encounter with aliens will place humanity and all of the life forms on this planet at great risk. If "they" can get here, they can kill us. Inviting more advanced civilizations to come hunting for us could mean the end of life on this planet. Professor Hawking's fear of space aliens while alarmist is not anywhere near as likely as asteroids destroying the planet. That in fact has happened before and without a space defense system this will happen again.

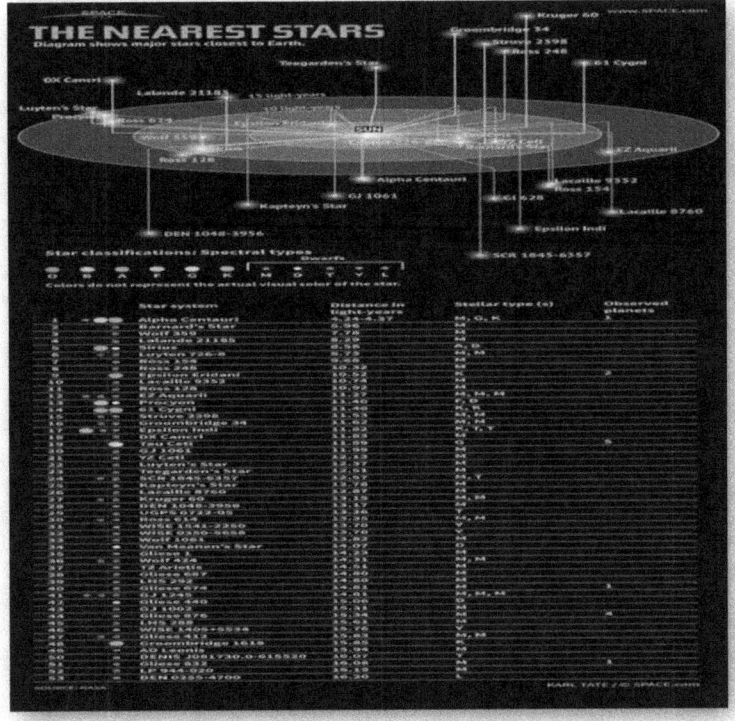

(Karl Tate courtesy of space.com)

From the horrific sins of my Spanish and Portuguese ancestors and the devastation of the indigenous people on this side of this very small planet to the current destruction of numerous species, we should expect the same treatment. Human history is one of genocide. Exterminating numerous indigenous people with disease as well as better weapons prevailed. Unless we work together as a planet, the same fate awaits us.

The Russians, Chinese, Indians, Americans, European Union and others have excellent scientists working in the defense sectors of their economies. This research work on weapons should be accelerated but it must be a joint effort. The danger to our Earth from asteroids can only be ignored at the peril of all life on our small planet.

Unlike the animal kingdom, humans do not have a contract with nature. When the lion is finished eating, the other animals will literally graze right next to the pride and not be bothered. They all understand that the meal has been provided. The lions do not kill off other animals for "sport" but only to eat what they need. Humans kill for the joy of killing, not because of necessity. Would we expect less of an alien civilization that had mastered the use of the atom for space travel? Hawkin's space aliens notwithstanding, the far bigger danger is from a collision with an asteroid that would end civilization.

It is not proven science that aliens have been in contact with human civilizations. It is the subject of much science fiction, and terrible documentaries. There is no science that human accomplishments were the result of instruction of space aliens. Must of these conjectures and poorly developed documentaries have been disproven by the scientific community. Still, it is important to develop space-based weapons and better propulsion systems for inter solar-system travel and protection of all life on this tiny planet. The clearest evidence our planet has not been visited by alien civilizations is we are still alive and not occupied.

The current Iron Dome and Missile Defense System that has been developed by the U.S. military and Israel needs to be expanded and deployed in outer space. A global space defense shield will protect the earth from asteroids. A global Iron Dome Missile Defense System needs to be deployed as soon as scientifically possible. Here, research must be accelerated and expanded with all military scientists working together. We all have a shared interest in survival. There are tens of thousands of asteroids just in our solar system. All it takes is one large asteroid and the present life forms on this tiny planet will be exterminated.

The 1950s and '60s brought a host of projects involving the use of nuclear power for space travel. Eventually, the projects were cancelled because of lack of progress and funding. The Americans have not been able to overcome the effects of radiation and the necessity for shielding, thus the extra weight made these scientific projects unfeasible. We gave up instead of continuing with the science of the use of atomic power for space travel. Research in this area should be re-started. New propulsion systems must be developed to reduce the massive distances between planets. The ocean of our ancestors seemed to go on forever. Technology improved and the distances between continents has been shortened from months to hours.

Given the distances of outer space where a Mars mission can take up to ten months, being able to get there in one week with the use of the power of the atom is something that should be pursued. The Russians have a program underway proposing the use of the atom for long distance space exploration.

Anatolij Perminov, head of the Russian Federal Space Agency, announced that it is going to develop a nuclear-powered spacecraft for deep space travel. Preliminary design was done by 2013, and nine more years are planned for development (in space assembly). The price is set at 17 billion rubles ($600 million). The nuclear propulsion would have mega-watt class, provided necessary funding is available, Roscosmos Head stated.

> "This system would consist of a space nuclear power and the matrix of ion engines. "…Hot inert gas temperature of 1500 °C from the reactor turns turbines. The turbine turns the generator and compressor, which circulates the working fluid in a closed circuit. The working fluid is cooled in the radiator. The generator produces electricity for the same ion (plasma) engine…"

He said the propulsion will be able to support human missions to Mars, with cosmonauts staying on the red planet for 30 days. This journey to Mars with nuclear propulsion and a steady acceleration would take six weeks, instead of eight months by using chemical propulsion – assuming thrust of 300 times higher than that of chemical propulsion.[6]

The world needs to put the tribal differences of the past aside and concentrate on the global threats to our planet's survival. This means we can look out to the universe and search for other life forms like scouts in ancient times observing the enemy. It means protecting the planet from an asteroid, something that will require global military cooperation. A space based system is too expensive for any one nation but with militaries working together, it is not outside of human capabilities.

Had the indigenous people of the Americas repelled every incursion of my Spanish and Portuguese ancestors as well as those of the northern European tribes, they would not have been slaughtered. Obviously the dinosaurs were not able to move the asteroid that had a collision with the earth that wiped them out. Alien civilizations are a very small threat to humanity but one we need to at least study. But asteroids are a clear and present danger to all life forms on this tiny planet.

The study of advanced weapons should continue for as long as humans occupy this planet. Scientific research on weapons and space travel is what will ultimately save mankind and our animal and plant kingdom from asteroids. We have bigger fights to prepare for than fighting each other. Religious books have their place, but asteroids could not care less about who owns what piece of land based upon 7,000-year-old texts.

We live in a new age. The planet has become tiny and international travel is a reality for millions of people. We live in a interconnected global world where we can talk with friends on the other side of the planet and with proper planning visit them. We can eat Thai food while we drink Argentine wine, wear Russian clothes, drive Japanese vehicles made with Spanish parts and Mexican labor and talk on cell phones made in China with Korean parts. We are one planet. Developing space based defense systems is just an insurance policy that present day life forms will not suffer the same fate as the dinosaurs.

1 International Standards Organization, ISO. More than almost any other organization, ISO has made us a smaller world. Trade takes place more efficiently with 16e nations all abiding with making their products and services safer. This organization works with regional organizations, scientists, governments and industry to create standards for industry, food, water and climate. This is one of the greatest legal achievements in human history. The organization works because the members believe in the system of law created by the framework set up globally. For more information, visit their website: " International Standards Organization. Accessed July 23, 2015. http://www.iso.org/iso/home.html.

2 "El Camino Real De Tierra Adentro." Wikipedia. Accessed July 23, 2015. http://en.wikipedia.org/wiki/El_Camino_Real_de_Tierra_Adentro.

3 "Stephen Hawking: Alien Life Is out There, Scientist Warns." The Telegraph. Accessed July 23, 2015. http://www.telegraph.co.uk/news/science/space/7631252/Stephen-Hawking-alien-life-is-out-there-scientist-warns.html.

4 "Brain, Marshall. "What If an Asteroid Hit the Earth?" HowStuffWorks. Accessed July 23, 2015. http://science.howstuffworks.com/nature/natural-disasters/asteroid-hits-earth.htm.

5 "Goldilocks Planet." Wikipedia. Accessed July 23, 2015. http://en.wikipedia.org/wiki/Goldilocks_planet.

6 "Russians to ride a nuclear-powered spacecraft to Mars." President Dmitry Medvedev says Russia will spend $600 million on a nuclear-powered spacecraft to take men to Mars, and beyond. Is it safe? By Fred Weir, Correspondent October 29, 2009 "Russians to Ride a Nuclear-powered Spacecraft to Mars." The Christian Science Monitor. Accessed July 23, 2015. http://www.csmonitor.com/World/Global-News/2009/1029/russians-to-ride-a-nuclear-powered-spacecraft-to-mars. See also: "Nuclear Pulse Propulsion." Wikipedia. Accessed July 23, 2015. https://en.wikipedia.org/wiki/Nuclear_pulse_propulsion.

PART II

Economics and
Exploration

CHAPTER 4

Exploration, Immigration and Population Growth

"The human race is likely to be wiped out by a doomsday virus . . . unless we set up colonies in space. Although Sept. 11th was horrible, it didn't threaten the survival of the human race like nuclear weapons do. . . . In the long term, I'm more worried about biology. Nuclear weapons need large facilities, but genetic engineering can be done in a small lab. The danger is that, either by accident or design, we create a virus that destroys us. I don't think the human race will survive unless we spread into space. There are too many accidents that can befall life on a single planet."
— PROFESSOR STEPHEN HAWKING

When the American West was explored, settled and developed, the growth opportunities were as vast as the prairies and as high as the mountains. From the early 1800s to today, both population and economic activity have grown. As the developed world's economies have matured, the rate of economic growth slowed. Trees eventually reach their natural size and stop growing. Animals reach maturity. This is a natural biological process. This is one reason why the United States and Western Europe have slow economic growth. The land has been explored, fully developed.

Absent exploration of the inner solar system and a careful exploration of the ocean floors, our country does not have new lands to conquer. We have conquered a continent. Now 500 years after my Spanish and Portuguese ancestors ventured forth into the unknown, cities like Chicago are home to more than three million people. Los Angeles and the surrounding suburbs have a population of over 10 million people. A continent that had large stable Native populations now has over 310 million people. With a global population that has exploded in the last 200 years, it is easy to see why we have an excess supply of unskilled and skilled labor.

Immigration from the 1500s to the start of the last century was east to west, primarily from Europe to the Americas. Today, immigration is primarily south to north from the belt near the equator to the United States, Canada and Europe. The problem is, with the exception of Canada, the excess labor cannot be absorbed by the fully developed economies of the United States and the European Union. Consequently, migrants drown at sea, are murdered by vicious gangs or die in the deserts of the Southwest trying to reach safer lands. Over-population and excess labor has made for a very crowded planet. There are no land areas for people to migrate like in times past. Economics is the heart of the problem with immigration. Labor is unwanted and has no home. Marx' "army of the unemployed" is a reality faced by all nations. What are we going to do with all of these workers?[1] Technological unemployment is a global reality.

Many countries do not allow any immigration. Japan has historically not allowed an already crowded country to take on new immigrants.[2] China with 1.3 billion people does not need more mouths to feed.[3] Russia is attracting labor from their former Soviet republics as their country's work force ages.[4] So where are all of these people going to work, live and how are they going to eat? Some countries have declining populations like the developed nations in the European Union and Japan, while others are still growing. Over-population has resulted in the earth's resources being stretched too thin.

As the world continues to add people at the rate of 70 to 100 million net per year, wildlife becomes extinct; water resources are in decline and pollution of every kind imaginable saturates an already polluted ocean.[5] In the last 500 years, we have explored all of the land areas on our small planet. Like each other or not we have to explore the inner solar system and carefully harness the resources under the waves.

When global exploration started in the 15th century, the planet had less than one billion people. From 1800 to 1930, our population doubled to slightly over two billion. In the last 100 years our population explosion has added another four billion people.

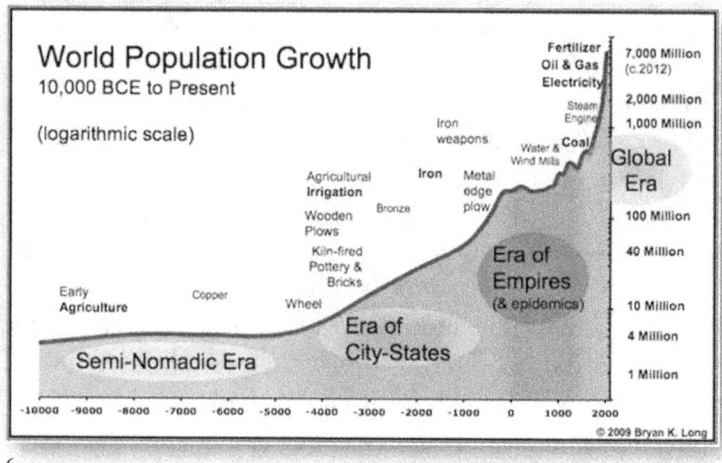

Immigration is in part a result of population growth. It will continue to be one of the most explosive political issues of this century. The political instability in the Middle East, North Africa and Central America resulted in people wanting to migrate to safer lands. While the political problems of war and instability and resulting immigration pressures is well known, policy planners are not proposing long-term solutions. Immigration was the traditional safety valve for government to deal with excess labor and poverty. "Send me your poor, huddled masses yearning to be free" is no longer an accepted slogan for unwelcome immigrants to the United States.

Some understanding of global demographics is imperative if we are realistically going to address environmental problems and shift resources toward space and ocean exploration. These problems are all intertwined and therefore must be studied together. According to the World Health Organization:

[T]he global average life expectancy is 70.5 years as of 2012, with women living an average of 73 years and men approximately 68 years. In 2010, the global fertility rate was estimated at 2.52 children per woman. ***

The nominal 2013 gross world product was estimated at US $74.31 trillion by the CIA, giving an annual global per capita figure of around US $10,500. Around 1.29 billion people (18.4% of the world population) live in extreme poverty, subsisting on less than US $1.25 per day; approximately 870 million people (12.25%) are undernourished, 83% of the world's over-15s are considered literate. In June 2014, there were around 3.03 billion global Internet users, constituting 42.3% of the world population.

The Han Chinese are the world's largest single ethnic group, constituting over 19% of the global population in 2011. The world's most-spoken first languages are Mandarin Chinese (spoken by 12.44% of the world's population), Spanish (4.85%), English (4.83%), Arabic (3.25%) and Hindustani (2.68%). The world's largest religion is Christianity, whose adherents account for 33.35% of the global population; Islam is the second-largest religion, accounting for 22.43%, and Hinduism the third, accounting for 13.78%. In 2005, around 16% of the global population were reported to be non-religious.[7]

From a historical perspective, 500 years is not a long time. So where are humans next going to migrate? Clearly the small planet does not have any land areas that need more people.

There are numerous projections on population growth and where the size of the number of people on the planet will end up. With urbanization and education the most likely scenario is the human population will stabilize at between 8 and 9 billion people. Educated women have fewer children but population growth will continue in the short run.

What this will mean for wildlife, climate change from the carbon releases into the atmosphere as well as the fish stocks seems precarious if not outright dangerous. This is one of the most compelling reasons why humans must explore the oceans and outer space and seek to colonize Mars as a second home.

Despite the impressive 500-year conquest of all land areas, the oceans have been overlooked. Why should we explore the oceans? Oceanographer and renowned scientist Dr. Marcia K. McNutt has a reasonable answer:

> "The desire to explore is fundamental to the human spirit. It is what inspires mountaineers to risk frostbite in scaling the highest peaks or malaria in penetrating the deepest jungles. The perils of any terrestrial exploration pale in comparison, however, to the challenges encountered in exploring the deep sea. The vast majority of ocean depths are bone chillingly cold (<2 degrees C), completely dark, and have ambient pressures equivalent to the weight of hundreds of atmospheres. Exploration of the deep sea, then, is impossible without a substantial investment in technology."[8]

The use of public funds for exploration is always controversial. The reason for the controversy is there is not an immediate return on investment from exploration to increase the public treasury. Exploration is a long-term investment — sometimes 50 or 100 years. Politics is a short-term profession where the concern is the next election. Properly funding exploration is difficult because of the nature of the people who run governments. Spending money on defense is a great way to keep known constituents happy, campaign contributions flowing and avoid taking a risk on something innovative.

Occasionally there will be a statesman like President Thomas Jefferson who had the foresight to realize the gains will arrive in the far distant future. His Louisiana Purchase doubled the size of the United States.

Historically, there have been people with the foresight to lead their countries despite not achieving immediate results. We have to be able to see the future in time spans longer than the next quarterly report or next election. Three months ahead in the corporate world and one election ahead in the political world make planning for solutions to the difficult problems facing the planet nearly impossible. We need the long-term view of saving humanity and the planet from certain destruction. Most people could care less about which political party runs the United States in this century. The concern is how the country is governed, not who is in power or what race or sex this person might be.

History is a good guide on what worked. The man chiefly responsible for Portugal's age of exploration and what eventually started European expansion into other parts of our small planet was Prince Henry, third son of King Jao I (John) and his English wife, Queen Philippa of Lancaster. Prince Henry was born in 1394. In 1419, his father made him governor of

Portugal's southernmost coasts. Under Henry's leadership, the Portuguese sent numerous expeditions down the west coast of Africa to outflank the Muslim hold on trade routes and to establish colonies.[9]

Superstitions being what they were, these expeditions moved slowly due to the mariners' belief that waters at the equator were at the boiling point, that human skin turned black and sea-monsters would engulf ships.[10] The benefits to Portugal came slowly. It wasn't until 27 years after Prince Henry's death that Bartolomeu Dias braved these "dangers" and rounded the Cape of Good Hope in 1487.[11]

What Henry is most famous for is establishing a naval observatory for the teaching of navigation, astronomy and cartography in about 1450.[12] Prince Henry never lived to see the tremendous benefits to Portugal and Europe from his school of navigation and his push for exploration of a route to India and China. This long-term policy was a very smart political move that gave the tiny country of Portugal an upper hand in the race for the trade routes to Asia and in becoming a global maritime power.

This push for exploration also resulted in the development of numerous new types of ships and technology for this small nation. Portugal made the push around Africa and into India and Asia. Their ships continued to evolve and the technology improved with every voyage. Portuguese explorer Vasco da Gama and others who followed him opened India and Asia to trade about 40 years after Prince Henry died.[13] The long-term effect of Portuguese maritime policy was history-making success.

Sometimes luck plays a large role in world events. Columbus first went to Portugal and lived there for several years, trying to convince the king to commission a voyage westward to the lucrative trade with Asia and India. When Columbus finally got his audience with King John II, the science advisors to the king recommended against the voyage. They believed his math was wrong and it was much farther than his estimates. History proved the Portuguese were correct.[14]

Having failed in Portugal, the Genoan sailor took his vision of a western voyage to India to the Spaniards. Finally, in 1492, Columbus sailed on three tiny ships into the unknown. Spain did not get an immediate benefit. It was not until 1524 — long after Queen Isabella and King Ferdinand had funded these expeditions — that Spain conquered the Aztecs and Incas.[15] Those of us who are older realize that 28 years is not a long time.

Spain temporarily became the most wealthy and powerful nation on the planet. Spain acquired so much gold from the Aztecs and silver from the Incas that these metals created fresh currency and fueled the start of the industrial revolution. Europeans achieved global dominance from their explorations and subsequent colonization of lands already occupied by various indigenous peoples. It was more by historical accident than by design. And but for a change in policy, China would have ruled the world.

From 1405 to 1433, Chinese Admiral Cheng Ho led an expedition of approximately 30,000 men and some of the largest wooden ships ever built on several voyages exploring the Pacific Rim, India and even into Africa in his service of Emperor Chu Ti. A change in leadership in China resulted in the cancellation of this exploration program and with it, Chinese conquest of the world.[16]

The Chinese had superior ships and equipment. Their flagship was larger than all three of Columbus' ships combined.[9]

They had the resources, the science and experience to defeat any navy on Earth. What they lacked was a leader with a vision of the future.

(Zheng He's treasure ship (four hundred feet) and Columbus's St. Maria (eighty-five feet) (Illustration by Jan Adkins, 1993.)

Maintaining this fleet was very expensive, given the other Chinese projects that were taking place during this same period. The new administration decided benefits were too far removed. That and infighting within the imperial court cancelled the program. The benefits of trade and colonies in other parts of the world was not in the vision of China's future when this very successful exploration program was suddenly cancelled.[17]

The Chinese government did not believe there was any reason for their subjects to travel abroad as the rest of the world was uncivilized. After canceling the program, they banned all travel abroad and the logs of the great explorer were destroyed.[18]

Political decisions become mistakes after time has tested the consequences. Spain soon squandered most of its immense wealth on various misguided military adventures. Spain failed to build a strong manufacturing base and imported finished products from other parts of Europe. This stimulated the economy of other countries but did not improve Spain's economic strength. The circulation of all of the gold and silver revived the commerce of the long-fallen Roman economy.

The exploration and subsequent acquisition of gold, silver and slaves did not mean Spain used its resources for long-term economic development. As individuals or as nations, how we use our wealth, whether stolen or earned, will determine our lot in life. Spain did not understand the long-term significance of her discoveries.

Being ruled by religious fanatics, eventually Spain lost her power and empire. Like the burning of the library at Alexandria and the subsequent loss of knowledge, some of the books of the Aztecs and Incas were burned by the Spaniards as "works of the devil". Superstition prevailed over rational scientific inquiry. With so much yet to be discovered, we can only hope religious extremists will not prevent scientific knowledge from going forward.

The oceans will be explored with or without the United States. The resources will be harnessed. New industries will be developed. Exploration and harnessing of the resources of the oceans will enable the United States to bring back industries that were mistakenly exported as a result of globalization. Either the United States will take this direction or it will be left behind by history and its economy will continue to stagnate. Eventually, the failure to explore will result in poverty. Eventually the military-industrial complex will become irrelevant to the problems facing humanity in this century.

There is no question people are going to get injured and die from the accidents that will happen when humans explore the oceans and the heavens. This does not mean we should eschew exploration. If anything, the inevitability of death should make life more adventurous. Exploration is dangerous — this is why we should do it. It's exciting.

---

1 See generally, "Reserve Army of Labour." Karl Marx was not the first to observe the problem of excess labor. One cannot properly understand a capitalist economic system without studying Marx. Marx, Karl. "Reserve Army of Labour."Wikipedia. Accessed July 23, 2015. http://en.wikipedia. org/wiki/Reserve_army_of_labour. See also "Das Kapital" Chapter 25. "Capitalistic accumulation itself… constantly produces, and produces in the direct ratio of its own energy and extent, a relatively redundant population of workers, i.e., a population of greater extent than suffices for the average needs of the valorisation of capital, and therefore a surplus-population… It is the absolute interest of every capitalist to press a given quantity of labour out of a smaller, rather than a greater number of labourers, if the cost is about the same… The more extended the scale of production, the stronger this motive. Its force increases with the accumulation of capital." Ibid.
2 Burgess, Chris. "Japan's 'no Immigration Principle' Looking as Solid as Ever | The Japan Times." Japan Times RSS. Accessed July 23, 2015. http://www.japantimes.co.jp/community/2014/06/18/voices/japans-immigration-principle-looking-solid-ever/#.VWAaNUvBduZ.
3 Boehler, Patrick. "Under China's New Immigration Law, Harsher Fines for Illegal Foreigners." South China Morning Post. July 1, 2013. Accessed July 23, 2015. http://www.scmp.com/news/china/article/1272959/under-chinas-new-immigration-law-harsher-fines-illegal-foreigners.
4 Malinkin, Mary Elizabeth. "Russia: The World's Second-Largest Immigration Haven."The National Interest. August 10, 2014. Accessed July 23, 2015. http://nationalinterest.org/blog/the-buzz/russia-the-worlds-second-largest-immigration-haven-11053?page=2.
5 Steck, Theodore L. "Human Population Explosion." Human Population Explosion. February 26, 2014. Accessed July 23, 2015. http://www.eoearth.org/view/article/153596/.
6 "World Population 2013…What Do We Now Know?" Efergy Blog. Accessed July 23, 2015. http://efergy.com/blog/world-population-2013-what-do-we-now-know/#.

7 "Demographics of the World." Wikipedia. Accessed July 23, 2015.
http://en.wikipedia.org/wiki/Demographics_of_the_world.

8 McNutt, Marcia, PhD. "Role of Technology in Ocean Exploration."
NOAA Ocean Explorer Podcast RSS. Accessed July 23, 2015. http://
oceanexplorer.noaa.gov/explorations/02davidson/background/technol-
ogy/technology.html.

9 "Henry the Navigator." Wikipedia. Accessed July 23, 2015. http://
en.wikipedia.org/wiki/Henry_the_Navigator. Ibid at: "HENRY OF
PORTUGAL THE NAVIGATOR PORTUGUESE MARINE EXPLORER
DUKE OF VISEU." HENRY OF PORTUGAL THE NAVIGATOR POR-
TUGUESE MARINE EXPLORER DUKE OF VISEU. Accessed July 23,
2015. http://www.solarnavigator.net/history/henry_the_navigator.htm.

10 "Bartolomeu Dias." History.com. Accessed July 23, 2015. http://
www.history.com/topics/exploration/bartolomeu-dias One. "Vasco Da
Gama." Wikipedia. Accessed July 23, 2015. http://en.wikipedia.org/
wiki/Vasco_da_Gama. te supra, 9.

11 Cite supra, 11.

12 See, "Christopher Columbus in Portugal 1476 to 1485. "In late 1483
or early 1484, he approached John II, the Portuguese king, for ships and
men to undertake the Atlantic voyage, offering to find Cipangu and India.
The king called in experts, including astronomers and mathematicians,
to judge the proposal. They turned Columbus down, believing that the
Atlantic distances involved were far greater than Columbus had estimated.
Nevertheless, John II secretly sent a vessel to test Columbus's theory; it
returned without reaching any shore." "Christopher Columbus Life in
Portugal 1476 to 1485." Christopher Columbus Life in Portugal 1476 to
1485. Accessed July 23, 2015. http://www.christopher-columbus.eu/
portugal-1476-1485.htm.

13 DiMarco, Violet. "Spanish Conquistadors." Spanish Conquistadors.
March 11, 2014. http%3A%2F%2Fwn.com%2Fcategory%3Aspanish_
conquistadors.

14 Hadingham, Evan. "Ancient Chinese Explorers." PBS. January 16,
2001. Accessed July 23, 2015. http://www.pbs.org/wgbh/nova/ancient/
ancient-chinese-explorers.html.

15 Ibid

CHAPTER 5

American Exploration and Protection of the Oceans

> "We must continue as a nation to set out
> for new frontiers, whether under the sea
> or into the heavens. We must continue to
> try to conquer the seemingly impossible --
> to discover the unimaginable, to find out
> more about what's out there, and in the
> process, about ourselves and what's here."
> — PRESIDENT BILL CLINTON, JUNE 12, 2000

There are some very dedicated private individuals and employees of the National Oceanic and Atmospheric Administration (NOAA) who want to explore and protect the vast oceans. For fiscal year 2016, the NOAA proposed a discretionary budget of $5,982,625,000, an increase of $533,716,000, or 9.8 percent above the 2015 adopted budget. [1] This $5.9 billion is less than one week of defense spending. Americans spend ten times this amount on their pets, over $58 billion annually.[2] Given that the federal budget is more than $3.8 trillion, $6 billion is not a lot of money.[3]

There are no major defense contractors with campaign contributions pushing Congress to build ships for exploration and harnessing the resources of the oceans. The motivation for a push in this area is the curiosity that makes humans venture forth into the unknown. This is where the U.S. Navy and its contractors can provide a tremendous service for all of mankind. By working with other nations and the United Nations, we can protect the oceans. Only with law will there be peace. Ocean pollution hurts humans, not just sea life. If fish ingest garbage, it's passed on to humans when we consume them.

In this century, we will not need 10 super Nimitz aircraft carrier battle groups to fight the Soviet Union on two continents. The threats in this century are from international killers and the destruction of the environment.

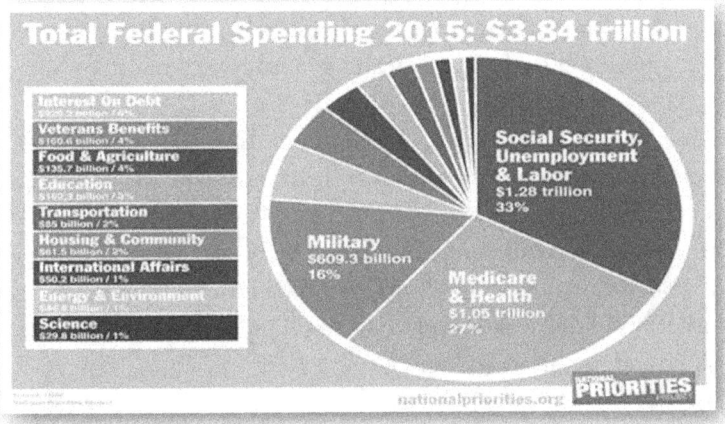

What will work in creating a new industrial base is building deep ocean exploration and mining vessels. For the cost of one Nimitz aircraft carrier battle group, all of the oceans can be properly explored.

One company stands out in the ability to build the vessels needed to properly explore the oceans. Huntington Ingalls Industries, ticker symbol HII, is the world's foremost builder of high-tech ships. In addition to building the Nimitz super carriers, this world-class company builds nuclear submarines and any other type of deep ocean vessel. In their words:

> "Huntington Ingalls Industries is America's largest military shipbuilding company and a provider of manufacturing, engineering and management services to the nuclear energy, oil and gas markets. For more than a century, HII's Newport News and Ingalls shipbuilding divisions in Virginia and Mississippi have built more ships in more ship classes than any other U.S. naval shipbuilder. Headquartered in Newport News, Virginia, HII employs approximately 38,000 people operating both domestically and internationally."[4]

This company is capable of creating entire new industries in ocean exploration. They employ thousands of people in several states. The company boasts building the "most complex ships in the world" and is the only builder of American aircraft carriers. It's one of two that builds nuclear-powered submarines, among other building credits, including amphibious assault ships, warships and missile destroyers."[5]

The oceans and space present a unique opportunity for global cooperation. All of humanity depends on the oceans for food. The Blue Planet is mysterious. It seems that once a week a new species is discovered. Shipwrecks with fortunes are recovered and great wealth lies under the seas.

Protecting the oceans for future generations is an immense job. However, the U.S. Navy and navy defense contractors are up to this task. Exploration and protection of the oceans gives the U.S. Navy a mission of global scope and a moral certainty to which people will be hard pressed to object. Each year more than a million sea birds and over 100,000 marine mammals and sea turtles suffer cruel deaths from becoming entangled in fishnets or suffocating in plastics.[6]

A plastic bag floats in the water off the coast of Pulau Bunaken, Indonesia.

The mission of protecting America from communism has been accomplished. A new and more important mission of global scope is to protect the oceans for all of mankind. The U.S. Navy can defeat all of the navies in the world combined in combat. But we are not fighting the navies of the entire world. Pollution, polluters, religious criminals and drug dealers are enemies of all mankind. They need to be stopped before more harm to our small planet is permanent.

Ocean exploration is an adventure. As Jacques Cousteau observed: "From birth man carries the weight of gravity on his shoulders. He is bolted to the Earth. But man has only to sink beneath the surface and he is free. Buoyed by water, he can fly in any direction — up, down, sideways — by merely flipping his hand. Under water, man becomes an archangel."[7]

The world has no choice regarding protection of the oceans. The British Petroleum Gulf of Mexico oil disaster of 2010 is the largest oil spill in world history. With deep sea oil drilling to provide an increasing population of over 7 billion people with fossil fuels, it is only a question of when there will be another disastrous oil spill. Obviously, using fossil fuels to provide power for our industrial systems is an environmentally flawed model. There are no easy answers, but the current system of oil and gas use in a world with an increasing population and diminishing resources will mean more deep-ocean drilling and more disastrous environmental results.

By redirecting defense spending toward preservation of the oceans and carefully harnessing resources, the United States will see immediate economic growth. Entire new industries will be developed around deep ocean mining, harnessing energy, protecting wildlife and even building hotels for visitors from above. Only the U.S. Navy and our navy defense contractors are ideally suited for the task of transitioning to protection of resources as well as deep ocean mining and energy development.

We have controlled the top of the waves for 60 years and kept the peace. Now it is time for the U.S. Navy and the navy defense contractors to have a new mission of global importance: Save the fish stock and protect the oceans as well as harness the resources under the waves.

Where now there is no demand for warships to fight enemies of the last century, millions of new jobs will be created in steel, engineering, biotech, computer sciences, oceanography, geology and numerous other fields. This will re-industrialize the country. Young people have the right to expect national policy to create a safe environment and a sound economy. This change in defense policy will work.

One individual who has succeeded in making some of the most spectacular movies ever decided to use his talent to personally explore the oceans. James Cameron is like the explorers of old. He is smart and brave. Inspired by Jacques-Yves Cousteau in his youth, Mr. Cameron has turned his attention to ocean exploration. He helped design and built a submarine that descended to the deepest place on the planet, the Mariana Trench off the coast of Guam. "Exploration comes with risk, but it is a risk that is worth something."[8]

His journey into the deep will be followed by other adventurers and entrepreneurs. Curiosity is what drives exploration. Now necessity requires a change in direction. The next administration needs to build ocean-going vessels to do what James Cameron, Jacques-Yves Cousteau, Ferdinand Magellan, James

Cook, and others have done. we need to explore, carefully preserve and develop the massive resources underneath the seas.

1 National Oceanic And Atmospheric Administration.

2 "Americans Spent a Record $56 Billion on Pets Last Year." CBSNews. Accessed July 23, 2015. http://www.cbsnews.com/news/americans-spent-a-record-56-billion-on-pets-last-year/.

3 "Policy Basics: Where Do Our Federal Tax Dollars Go?" Policy Basics: Where Do Our Federal Tax Dollars Go? Accessed July 23, 2015. http://www.cbpp.org/research/policy-basics-where-do-our-federal-tax-dollars-go.

4 "Who We Are." Huntington Ingalls Industries:. Accessed July 23, 2015. http://www.huntingtoningalls.com/about/index.

5 Ibid.

6 By Laura Parker, National Geographic PUBLISHED July 16, 2014. "First of Its Kind Map Reveals Extent of Ocean Plastic." National Geographic. Accessed July 23, 2015. http://news.nationalgeographic.com/news/2014/07/140715-ocean-plastic-debris-trash-pacific-garbage-patch/.and see also: "Plastic Pollution." Plastic Pollution. Accessed July 23, 2015. http://coastalcare.org/2009/11/plastic-pollution/.

7 "Jacques-Yves Cousteau." - Wikiquote. Accessed July 23, 2015. http://en.wikiquote.org/wiki/Jacques-Yves_Cousteau.

8 "DEEPSEA CHALLENGE." DEEPSEA CHALLENGE. Accessed July 23, 2015. http://www.deepseachallenge.com/.

CHAPTER 6

The Law of the Seas

> "The law approximates a body of rules
> that are approximately enforced"
> — Dr. Francis D. Wormuth

Although the public has been losing confidence in the American legal system, it works the majority of the time. There are anomalies and difficult cases will on occasion make bad law. On the whole, the American legal system works. It is not equipped to deal with failed social or political policies, like the war on drugs or to stop the collapse of the fish stocks or reliance on fossil fuels. These are policies that require national and international leadership from all parts of the political spectrum. Political parties, not just lawyers, need to address the environmental problems of pollution, the collapsing fish stocks and climate change.

Given the disparities between rich, powerful nations and the poor and powerless, our global society needs law to protect the weak from the strong. This includes protecting global wildlife with international conventions and treaties. The nations of the world have come together and worked out a comprehensive international agreement on the laws of the oceans. The legal framework developed important international rules of conduct on fisheries, mammals and the environment. With proper global enforcement, there is a chance at success.

With an exploding population of over 7 billion and no world government to protect them, the sea creatures are in harm's way. As author Jonette N. Braathen has observed:

"With the convention of most of the world's nations at the United Nations Conference on Environment and Development (UNCED) in Rio de Janeiro, Brazil, in 1992, the environmental issues was put high on the political agenda. This was a major event in the process of integrating environmental concern in all sectors - including the fisheries sector. This implies that decision-making in the fisheries sector does not only involve the actual fisheries, but also the consequences and implications for the environment as such. In addition, the fisheries sector is becoming the focus of environmental organizations with a rising concern for the management of marine recourses. Consequently, there is a increasing need for co-operation between fisheries and environmental experts and governments to safeguard the interests of both sectors and their mutual interest in a sound environment and the sustainable management of marine recourses."[1]

Years of negotiation and compromise resulted in numerous agreements to protect the water and wildlife resources of the planet. The end result is the Convention on the Law of the Sea. This historic agreement was the result of years of work and negotiations between numerous and diverse nations of our global community. The history of this important legal agreement that seeks to stop the damage to the oceans originated with the efforts of many people. Among the most important was Arvid Pardo.

On 1 November 1967, Malta's Ambassador to the United Nations, Arvid Pardo, asked the nations of the world to look around them and open their eyes to a looming conflict that could devastate the oceans, the lifeline of man's very survival.

"It is the only alternative by which we can hope to avoid the escalating tension that will be inevitable if the present situation is allowed to continue," he said.[2]

In the words of the United Nations,

"The Convention on the Law of the Sea (UNCLOS) sets out the legal framework within which all activities in the oceans and seas must be carried out. The legal order established by the Convention is balanced, sound and comprehensive. It provides a basis for the settled order of the oceans and seas for the foreseeable future. The Convention entered into force on 16 November 1994 and over the past years has achieved nearly universal acceptance. As of 2015, 162 countries and the European Union have joined the Convention and were bound by it."[3]

The provisions are fairly straightforward, see infra.[4] The nations of the world simply recognized a set of laws had to be developed to protect the ocean from the most dangerous predator, people. The convention, which attempts to govern the behavior of all 185 members of the United Nations, has not been ratified by the richest and most powerful, the United States of America.

The main criticisms of the law of the sea conventions come from the limitations on big business' ability to pursue economic development of the oceans. As the CATO Institute observed:

> The LOST (Law Of Sea Treaty) may purport to promote international justice, fairness, and cooperation, but in fact it advances none of those principles. Rather, it raises to the status of international law self-indulgent claims of ownership to be secured through an oligarchy of international bureaucrats, diplomats, and lawyers. And the treaty's specific provisions, mandating global redistribution of resources, creating a monopolistic public mining entity, restricting competition, and requiring the transfer of technology, reflect the sort of statist panaceas that were discredited by the demise of Soviet-style communism.[5]

The CATO Institute is one of the best in the world at opposing the growth of government. However, the spread of law to a lawless world is far different than creating a bureaucratic nightmare that will hinder big business. The exploration of the oceans needs to go forward. The economic development needs to be accomplished in a far different manner than the mining that took place in the 1800s and 1900s in the western United States. The colossal environmental damage from mining and dumping mining waste that was acceptable behavior before we had environmental laws is not something we wish to repeat in this century. Unregulated ocean mining and oil development destroy fragile sea life.

We can harvest the vast resources of the oceans. But we do not need to be reckless and indifferent in our approach. If any of you have ever seen the streams below the hard rock mines that were killed by mill tailings and industrial waste, you would be reluctant to repeat this damage on a world-wide scale under the seas. The last two centuries saw mining activity that was dangerous to humans and destructive of the environment.

As the Natural Resources Defense Council observed about the environmental problems created by Appalachian coal mining:

- Just one mountaintop removal mine can lay bare up to 10 square miles and pour hundreds of millions of tons of waste material into as many as a dozen "valley fills" -- some of which are 1,000 feet wide and a mile long.
- The explosive charges used in removal mining shake and crack homes, destroy drinking water supplies and can roll huge rocks onto homes, cars, property and public roads.
- Over the last 30 years, only a fraction of the millions of acres of land that coal mining has disturbed nationwide have been reclaimed to even minimum standards -- and the habitat and biodiversity that has been lost can never be fully restored.
- A total of 1,200 square miles of Appalachian forests will be gone by 2012, according to government projections. More than 300,000 acres of hardwood forests

have been destroyed or contaminated in West Virginia alone.

More than 1,200 miles of U.S. streams and rivers were destroyed or polluted by coal mining in central Appalachia over a 10-year span. If strung together, those polluted waterways would equal roughly half the length of the Mississippi River.[6]

Development of the oceans should take place as the extra four billion people we have added since 1940 will need resources to survive. However, economic development should not be accomplished on a "winner take all," the undersea environment be damned attitude like we had in the Wild West. That gold rush attitude was devastating to the environment.

An international framework of laws governing ocean exploration and development ultimately helps the United States. Then-retired Sen. Clairborne Pell throughout his career argued strenuously to ratify this important international treaty. In his words:

Mr. President, my delegation has the honor to introduce resolution A/53/L.45, entitled, "Large-scale pelagic drift-net fishing, unauthorized fishing in zones of national jurisdiction and on the high seas, fisheries by-catch and discards, and other developments." Once again, we would like to extend our gratitude to all those delegations who offered valuable suggestions and worked in a spirit of cooperation to draft this text.[7]

President Clinton was not successful in getting the United States Senate to ratify this treaty. The Bush administration was preoccupied with a war on Iraq and did not move to make this treaty legally binding on the world's most powerful nation. The pollution of the oceans and the destruction of the fisheries and sea mammals continues. The world's population keeps expanding and the message of consumerism and materialism is the song of the day on Wall Street and Madison Ave.

As of 2015, President Obama has not been successful in getting the U.S. Senate to ratify this important treaty. It needs to be a major political issue in the next election cycle. In the meantime, the fish stocks continue to be decimated and plastic continues to infest every part of the ocean. As the world's largest economy, we also create the most pollution and consume the most resources. It is time to lead and ratify this treaty.

American leadership in this century requires concerted action with the global community to revive the fish stocks and clean the oceans. The United States needs to ratify the Law of the Seas Convention. Governments, the fishing and tourist industries and non-profits can all work together to turn the collapse of the fish stocks around. This is not impossible; it just takes public awareness of the problems and proposed solutions.

There are some excellent organizations out there working hard to protect our fragile environment and make changes in consumption. Conservation International works all over the world. Its Chief Executive Officer, Peter Seligmann, explained why we have to invest in protecting nature. Gathering data will be essential to protecting our tiny planet.

"This investment in gathering, synthesizing and sharing new data is necessary for creating a society that can weather the pressures of change. Over the next century, the world's population will grow to over 9 billion people. We will double our demand for food, energy and water, and the changing climate will continue to exacerbate the uncertainties we face. Nature is the most cost-effective source we have to meet these demands. Monitoring its health will be key to ensuring a continual supply of the natural capital it provides to all of us."[8]

Adopting the Law of the Seas Convention by the United States can turn around the decline of the fish stocks and reverse the environmental damage being inflicted on the oceans. This is can be accomplished with the creation of a Global High Seas Marine Preserve.

---

1 Braathen, Jonette N. "International Co-operation on Fisheries and Environment." Google Books. Accessed July 24, 2015. https://books. google.com/books?id=TyXUvLh2DF0C&pg=PA5&lpg=PA5&dq =1.%09Braathen%2C%2BJonette%2BN.%2B%22International% 2BCo-operation%2Bon%2BFisheries%2Band%2BEnvironment.%2-2&source=bl&ots=HM3644EMxS&sig=gdJx26gZC0IDp3IW1As08BuX yPg&hl=en&sa=X&ved=0CB4Q6AEwAGoVChMI0M-d7qLzxgIVA32I Ch1KlQSh#v=onepage&q=1.%09Braathen%2C%20Jonette%20N.%20 %22International%20Co-operation%20on%20Fisheries%20and%20 Environment.%22&f=false.
2 "Overview - Convention & Related Agreements." UN News Center. Accessed July 24, 2015. http://www.un.org/Depts/los/convention_agreements/convention_historical_perspective.htm#Key%20provisions.
3 "United States Non-ratification of the UNCLOS." Wikipedia. Accessed July 24, 2015. http://en.wikipedia.org/wiki/United_States_non-ratification_of_the_UNCLOS.

4 "Overview - Convention & Related Agreements." UN News Center. Accessed July 24, 2015. http://www.un.org/depts/los/convention_agreements/convention_historical_perspective.htm#Key%20provisions.

5 Bandow, Doug. "Do Not Endorse the Law of the Sea Treaty." Do Not Endorse the Law of the Sea Treaty. January 27, 1994. Accessed July 24, 2015. http://www.cato.org/pubs/fpbriefs/fpb-029.html.

6 "Moving Mountains for Dirty Coal." http%3A%2F%2Fwww.nrdc.org%2Fenergy%2Fcoal%2Fmtr%2Fabout.asp.

7 http://ugspace.ug.edu.gh/handle/123456789/3001.

8 Seligmann, Peter. "'Big Data' Is an Investment in Nature -- and Human Well-being." The Huffington Post. Accessed July 24, 2015. http://www.huffingtonpost.com/peter-seligmann/big-data-is-an-investment_b_4474724.html.

CHAPTER 7

The Global High Seas
Marine Preserve

"The fate of the living planet is the most
important issue facing mankind."
— GAYLORD NELSON

N ational interests and greed often compete with global interests. The collapse of the fish stocks is a global problem that can be solved. Commercial interests subsidized by national governments who don't care about the collapse of the fish stocks will ruin it for the rest of us. Failure will affect all future generations. We don't have to like each other; but like each other or not we have no choice but to stop the slaughter of the oceans. The reality is humans need the fish from the oceans for food. As the Pew Charitable Trust Global Ocean Legacy observed on their website:

"The ocean covers nearly three-fourths of the globe and is home to nearly half of the world's known species, with countless yet to be discovered. Producing almost half of the oxygen in the atmosphere, it also absorbs vast amounts of carbon dioxide. The ocean helps support more than 250 million people who depend directly or indirectly on fishing for their livelihoods, and provides the main source of animal protein to more than 2.6 billion people. The oceans play an essential role in sustaining life on our planet, but human activities are increasingly threatening their health. Research shows that very large, fully protected marine reserves are key to rebuilding species abundance and diversity and protecting the overall health of the marine environment."[1]

Tens of thousands of people and hundreds of organizations all over the world are aware of the problems created by overfishing. Many organizations are working to stop the slaughter of the oceans' fisheries. What is working globally is the creation of marine preserves to revive the fish stocks and create healthy oceans. Amending the Law of the Seas Convention and creating a Global High Seas Marine Preserve that is off limits to commercial fishing forever will save the fish stocks. The other choice is extinction.

A marine preserve is a protected ocean area like a national park. It is off limits to development and to commercial fishing. When you travel to the Florida Keys, the fish are protected by the Florida Keys National Marine Sanctuary. This beautiful marine preserve is jointly operated by the National Ocean Atmospheric Administration and the State of Florida. Fishermen are able to recreationally fish, divers can visit the coral reefs and ship wrecks, as well as enjoy the beauty of protected oceans.

Contrast that national marine preserve with the fish stocks on the eastern coast of Florida. When you fish off the pier at Deerfield, Florida, you might catch a sunburn and if lucky maybe you will get one bite or two. The fish are few and the beaches are full of people. Between polluted oceans and overfishing, fish stocks globally are in big trouble.

(National Oceanic and Atmospheric Administration website)

The Office of National Marine Sanctuaries is the trustee for a network of 14 marine protected areas encompassing more than 170,000 square miles of marine and Great Lakes waters from Washington state to the Florida Keys, and from Lake Huron to American Samoa.[2]

As of 2014, there are over 6,500 protected marine areas on our small planet. These protected areas represent less then 3 percent of the ocean.[3] With over 97 percent of the oceans available for huge fishing vessels armed with 40 mile nets, radar, sonar, small planes as spotters and miles and miles of long lines, it is not a fair fight. The fish stocks are being slaughtered like the passenger pigeon and the buffalo. This slaughter can and must be stopped. The fish stocks can be revived. It is a winnable battle.

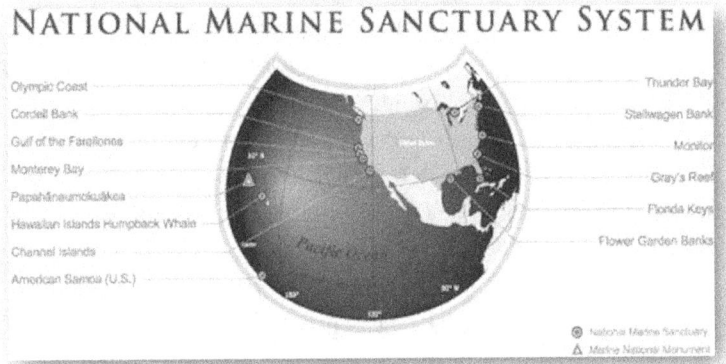

NATIONAL MARINE SANCTUARY SYSTEM

Olympic Coast
Cordell Bank
Gulf of the Farallones
Monterey Bay
Papahānaumokuākea
Hawaiian Islands Humpback Whale
Channel Islands
American Samoa (U.S.)

Thunder Bay
Stellwagen Bank
Monitor
Gray's Reef
Florida Keys
Flower Garden Banks

Pacific Ocean

National Marine Sanctuary
Marine National Monument

The network includes a system of 13 national marine sanctuaries and the Papahanaumokuakea Marine National Monument.[4]

There is hope. Unlike the military-industrial complex or the firearms lobby, the Fishing Industrial Complex is not very powerful. The fishing industry as a whole is not a very large business. Without government subsidies, these industries can't compete. According to CNN International:

"The worldwide fishing industry employs around 200 million people, generating $80 billion a year. But a hefty chunk of the industry's revenues come from subsidies, which are currently estimated at around $34 billion a year. Those most responsible for subsidizing the fishing industry are Japan (spending $5.3 billion a year), the European Union ($3.3 billion) and China ($3.1 billion), according to activist group Oceana."[5]

This is not a huge industry compared to the giants of commerce out there in the global economic jungle. Retail global giant Wal-Mart has gross revenues of over $480 billion. Industrial giant General Electric has gross revenues of over $144 billion. Defense giant Lockheed Martin has gross revenues of over $45 billion.[6] Commercial fishing companies would not survive without government subsidizes. Banning government subsidies globally and creating a Global High Seas Marine Preserve the fish stocks can be saved. This is an environmental fight we can win.

Closing off the high seas to commercial fishing will allow humans to continue to harvest fish by careful regulation of the catch. It will not mean the end of fish consumption. Each government can then best protect their fisheries as the United States and other nations are trying. What it will accomplish is save the fisheries as a food source.

World-reknowned scientist Dr. Daniel Pauly describes what has happened to the fish stocks as follows:

> Our oceans have been the victims of a giant Ponzi scheme, waged with Bernie Madoff–like callousness by the world's fisheries. Beginning in the 1950s, as their operations became increasingly industrialized — with onboard refrigeration, acoustic fish-finders, and, later, GPS — they first depleted stocks of cod, hake, flounder, sole, and halibut in the Northern Hemisphere. As those stocks disappeared, the fleets moved southward, to the coasts of developing nations and, ultimately, all the way to the shores of Antarctica, searching for icefishes and rockcods, and, more recently, for small, shrimplike krill. As the bounty of coastal waters dropped, fisheries

moved further offshore, to deeper waters. And, finally, as the larger fish began to disappear, boats began to catch fish that were smaller and uglier — fish never before considered fit for human consumption. Many were renamed so that they could be marketed: The suspicious slimehead became the delicious orange roughy, while the worrisome Patagonian toothfish became the wholesome Chilean seabass. Others, like the homely hoki, were cut up so they could be sold sight-unseen as fish sticks and filets in fast-food restaurants and the frozen-food aisle.

The scheme was carried out by nothing less than a fishing-industrial complex — an alliance of corporate fishing fleets, lobbyists, parliamentary representatives, and fisheries economists. By hiding behind the romantic image of the small-scale, independent fisherman, they secured political influence and government subsidies far in excess of what would be expected, given their miniscule contribution to the GDP of advanced economies — in the United States, even less than that of the hair salon industry. In Japan, for example, huge, vertically integrated conglomerates, such as Taiyo or the better-known Mitsubishi, lobby their friends in the Japanese Fisheries Agency and the Ministry of Foreign Affairs to help them gain access to the few remaining plentiful stocks of tuna, like those in the waters surrounding South Pacific countries.

Beginning in the early 1980s, the United States, which had not traditionally been much of a fishing country, began heavily subsidizing U.S. fleets, producing its own

fishing-industrial complex, dominated by large pro-
cessors and retail chains. Today, governments provide
nearly $30 billion in subsidies each year — about one-
third of the value of the global catch — that keep fisheries going, even when they have overexploited their
resource base. As a result, there are between two and
four times as many boats as the annual catch requires,
and yet, the funds to "build capacity" keep coming.[7]

The result of industrial harvesting of fish by giant vessels like
the massive Atlantic Dawn is one cause of the current collapse of the world's fisheries. It is reminiscent of the slaughter of the buffalo when railroads made their way across the
continent. When faced with the reality of extinction, some
forward-thinking individuals saved the buffalo. Where once
buffalo herds were massive and in the millions, humans almost made them extinct.

The same thing happened with whales. Without the hard
work of conservationists, every last whale in the oceans would
have been hunted to extinction. Mountain gorillas and other
large apes, too, would be extinct but for the efforts of brave
individuals like Jane Goodall and numerous others. It takes
courage to stand up against the forces of greed and at times
sheer stupidity. The planet has concerned individuals like environmentalist Jane Goodall, scientist Dr. Daniel Pauly, director
and adventurer James Cameron, actor Harrison Ford; hundreds
of non-profit organizations, government agencies and tens of
thousands of workers and millions of citizens globally that care
about the environment.[8]

Stopping giant commercial fishing vessels from slaughtering the fish stocks can be accomplished with public participation

and political will. If millions of citizens demand that the fish stocks be saved from collapse, political leaders will create a Global High Seas Marine Preserve. Politicians don't lead, they follow. Citizens need to lead their politicians in the right direction and force change from the bottom up. Like all social movements, it will not happen from the top down. If citizens hold public protests of commercial fishing vessels and boycott the purchase of endangered fish, the slaughter will stop. Here is where the consumer and government, not the commercial fishing companies, have power. Nobody is forcing anyone to buy fish that are going to become extinct from overfishing. If there is no profit in fishing, these companies will stop fishing.

As Charles Clover observed, "Atlantic Dawn is the greatest fish killing machine the world has ever seen."[9]

(Charles Clover online at: http://britishseafishing.
co.uk/atlantic-dawn-the-ship-from-hell/)

The collapse of the fisheries resulted by pursuit of short-term profits rather than the long-term survival of the fish stocks. These huge commercial fishing vessels are emptying out the oceans. Governments know about the slaughter. Politicians get money to be elected. They take money from the highest bidder, including campaign contributions from the fishing industry. In return, politicians provide subsidies to a fish industry that is too large for the number of fish being harvested from the oceans. The result is overfishing. Politicians can be voted out of office. If the fish stocks become extinct, they cannot be voted back to life. Politicians have the same data as the scientific community. They just don't care if the fish stocks collapse. If you like sea food then you need to vote these individuals out of office.

Another reason extremist politicians will not work to stop the slaughter of the fish stocks and are not concerned about environmental issues is their religious beliefs. Some extremist politicians believe the problems facing the planet are signs of "the end of times". Consequently trying to solve any of these problems is going against "God's will". The "End of Time" politicians don't care about the future of the Earth because they don't believe there will be a future. As Glenn Scherer observed:

> "People under the spell of such potent prophecies cannot be expected to worry about the environment. Why care about the earth when the droughts, floods, and pestilence brought by ecological collapse are signs of the Apocalypse foretold in the Bible? Why care about global climate change when you and yours will be rescued in the Rapture? And why care about converting from oil to solar when the same God who performed

the miracle of the loaves and fishes can whip up a few billion barrels of light crude with a Word?"[10]

When democracies elect people with no regard for the health and wellbeing of the planet, of course the fish stocks are going to collapse. This can all be changed with votes.

The collapse of the fish stocks is best exemplified by the decline of the jack mackerel. Having fished out the Mediterranean and the North Atlantic and been banned from destroying the protected fish stocks of the United States, the fleets of Europe and Asia are attacking the jack mackerel in full force. The result of greed, political ineptness and mismanagement is that a natural resource becomes extinct. As Mort Rosenblum and Mar Cabra reported in a New York Times story:

"It's going fast," he said as he looked at the 57-foot boat. "We've got to fish harder before it's all gone." Asked what he would leave his son, he shrugged: "He'll have to find something else."

Jack mackerel, rich in oily protein, is manna to a hungry planet, a staple in Africa. Elsewhere, people eat it unaware; much of it is reduced to feed for aquaculture and pigs. It can take more than five kilograms, more than 11 pounds, of jack mackerel to raise a single kilogram of farmed salmon.

Stocks have dropped from an estimated 30 million metric tons to less than a tenth of that in two decades. The world's largest trawlers, after depleting other oceans, now head south toward the edge of Antarctica to compete for what is left.

An eight-country investigation of the fishing industry in the southern Pacific by the International
Consortium of Investigative Journalists shows how the
fate of the jack mackerel may foretell the progressive
collapse of fish stocks in all oceans.

In turn, the fate of this one fish reflects a bigger picture: decades of unchecked global fishing pushed by geo-
political rivalry, greed, corruption, mismanagement and
public indifference. Daniel Pauly, an eminent University
of British Columbia oceanographer, sees jack mackerel
in the southern Pacific as an alarming indicator.

"This is the last of the buffaloes," he said. "When
they're gone, everything will be gone.".[11]

Unlike the massive military-industrial complex and the $1 tril-
lion defense budget, the fishing industry is tiny. This problem can
be solved by giving the world's navies a new mission, protect
the high seas from illegal commercial fishing. While this is being
done, expand the network of marine preserves globally from less
than 3 percent of the ocean to at least 70 percent with the creation of a Global High Seas Marine Preserve. Limit the size of fish
catch by quotas approved by scientists, not politicians or industry.

The collapse of the fish stocks is the result of numerous
historical forces all coming together at once. The human population increased from 1 billion in 1800 to over 7 billion in 2015.
In the same 200 year time frame, technology vastly improved.
As technology developed, the natural world was slaughtered.
Ancient trees were no match for chain saws, power blades, bull
dozers, explosives and saw mills. Buffalo and whales cannot
possibly fight back against gunpowder and bullets.

By the year A.D.1800 in the Western calendar, human population was exploding. Yet there was wilderness; numerous areas of the planet were unexplored. Whaling was an industry that had not yet driven these species to the brink of extinction. Buffalo were hunted and used for food and furs. Numerous indigenous nations still had territory that they could defend. European powers still had global empires and cultures were distinctly different. There were few cities on the planet with over one million people. No city had electricity. Automobiles, planes and coal-fired power plants did not exist. Nuclear power was not even an idea. Global fish stocks were healthy. The ancient forests of giant Redwoods and Sequoias were largely intact. Wolves and grizzlies still roamed the mountains and plains of America.

Globally, the mountain gorillas had their own vast territories along with the wild elephants, and tens of thousands of other species. Humans lived near these wild animals but were not yet able to slaughter them to extinction.

Today, a simple creature like a tuna fish cannot possibly survive against a modern killing machine like the giant fishing vessels. It has never been a fair fight between modern technology and the natural world. It is like a human armed with a bow and arrow up against a F-22 fighter or a redwood against a chainsaw. Time from a historical perspective is short. Approximately 500 years ago, in the time of Columbus there were millions of sea turtles. Their sound could be heard from miles off shore. A mere 200 years ago the oceans were filled with numerous types of fish.

As population increased and technology improved, fish stocks collapsed.

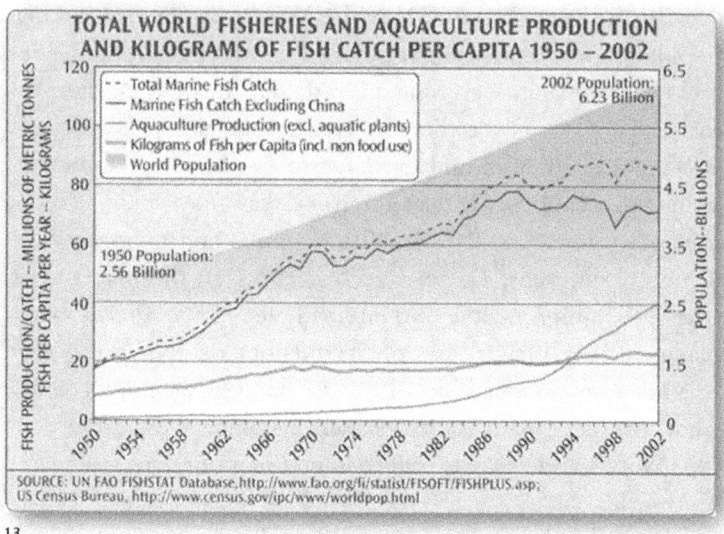

(Source: UN FAO Fishstat Database, http://www.
fao.org/fi/statis/FISOFT/FISHPLUS.asp
U.S. Census Bureau, http://www.census.gov/ipc/www/worldpop.html)

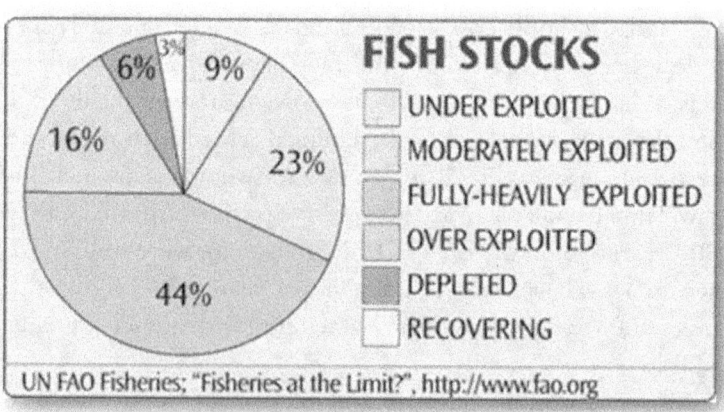

"75% of the major marine fish stocks are either depleted, over-exploited or being fished at their biological limit." [14]

The legal framework already exists under international law to create these marine preserves. The 1958 International Convention on Fishing and Conservation of Living Resources of the High Seas includes the following provision:

Article 4

1. If the nationals of two or more States are engaged in fishing the same stock or stocks of fish or other living marine resources in any area or areas of the high seas, these States shall, at the request of any of them, enter into negotiations with a view to prescribing by agreement for their nationals the necessary measures for the conservation of the living resources affected. [15]

The Obama administration was not able to obtain the cooperation of Congress on the important issue of preserving the fish stocks. Consequently, President Obama took the initiative. He increased the size of the Pacific Remote Islands National Monument established by President George W. Bush. America's largest marine preserve was made six times larger. Marine preserves protect the entire ecosystem of the oceans. [17] Increasing the size of this National Monument did not generate much media attention. Few fishermen venture out into this area, probably because it is not a major fishing site.

What the administration failed to do was seize the opportunity and call an international conference on the oceans and create a Global High Seas Marine Preserve. "The worst culprits contributing to this crisis are developed countries, with their vast fleets and technological prowess. Ten countries — Japan, South Korea, Taiwan, Spain, the United States, Chile, China, Indonesia, the Philippines, and France, in descending order – account for 70 percent of the fishing by value in the high seas".[17]

Because technological limitations no longer limit the ability to fish, a Global High Seas Marine Preserve is an excellent global policy change to revive entire ecosystems. The U.S. Navy, working with other nations, has the ability to patrol it and keep these preserves free from poachers. Absent people foregoing fish as food, a Global High Seas Marine Preserve patrolled by the world's navies is the best solution to reviving the fish stocks.

The power of the consumer can force substantive change. The United States, Canada and Mexico, the three North American Free Trade Agreement (NAFTA) nations, form the largest economy on the planet with a combined GDP of over $19 trillion dollars.[18] The European Union is the second largest economic power with a combined GDP of over $18 trillion dollars.[19] The two world's largest markets can put significant pressure on any nation to comply with accepted global rules of behavior. Here the public can help out by boycotting nations' products that refuse to quit overfishing and destroying the oceans.

Consumer boycotts work. When enough people put economic pressure on South Africa, as well as the hard work of Nelson Mandela and others, the evils of apartheid finally ended. The ultimate power to create change always lies with the individual in a consumer-based economy.

The United States must take the leadership role on this issue. But this is not possible if the United States refuses to ratify the Convention on the Law of the Seas discussed earlier. We cannot expect other nations to comply with international law if our nation refuses to be bound by the same rules.

There are inexpensive solutions to the fish stock collapse problem. The United States can initiate a global education campaign on overfishing and the consequences. Advertising can be donated by the major media conglomerates and the ads can be produced by environmental groups and research universities. Huge retail chains like Wal-Mart and Kroger can insist on sustainable catch. Consumers can help by only purchasing ocean safe seafood and not eating Ahi tuna, sea bass and other endangered species.

To accomplish the removal of the fishing vessels, the world's governments are going to have to initiate condemnation proceedings and purchase them from their owners. Governments are going to have to provide unemployment insurance for the fishing crews who will temporarily lose their jobs. The developed world will have to help these countries with foreign aid to offset this financial loss by the fishermen. It is clearly something we can accomplish with governments and non-government organizations working together.

Only a small handful of truly massive fishing vessels exist. According to the United Nation's Food and Agriculture Organization (FAO), there are less than 30,000 industrial size commercial fishing vessels in the world. Of these, approximately 15,000 belong to China.[20]

These huge fishing vessels are not part of the fishing that is done in traditional societies who depend on the oceans for nutrition. The expensive ocean-going industrial fishing vessels belong to a handful of countries and companies. The indigenous fishermen who feed their families do not use giant ocean-going vessels complete with sonar and massive industrial nets and freezers. They use traditional fishing techniques that do not drive species to extinction.

Good governance, public awareness and responsible industry practices can turn this around. As the FAO observed in its outlook on the future of the global fish stocks:

> "The future of the fisheries and aquaculture sector will be influenced by its capacity to address strategic interconnecting challenges of global and local relevance. Population and income growth, together with urbanization and dietary diversification, are expected to create additional demand for animal products, including fish in developing countries. Thus, the future of the sector will be the result of social development, in its ecological, social and economic contexts, at local, regional and global scales."[21]

There are some successes in stopping the slaughter of the oceans. The tiny nation of Kiribati has banned all commercial fishing in an area the size of California.[22] This tiny country is taking on the global fishing industry by creating the world's largest marine park to help the wildlife recover. When the smallest countries on the planet decide to protect their wildlife, the largest countries can also choose the moral high ground and stop the slaughter of the oceans. A problem faced by small countries is protecting the marine preserves. They don't have powerful navies and sufficient patrol vessels.

Again, the best protection of the fish in the world's oceans is to expand national marine preserves and make the high seas off limits to commercial fishing. This proposal to make the high seas off limits is being made by numerous international organizations. That move is long overdue and the world is finally moving in that direction. The world's navies can help small nations and enforce this ban to help revive the fish stocks.

Dr. Daniel Pauly, the world's foremost scholar on fisheries, said this about the initiative to close the high seas:

"The expansion of the law of the seas is not on the agenda of any country. It's an idea whose time has not yet come. It has only recently been proposed. It will take one to two decades."

"But if we continue with business as usual, I am afraid that the fish stocks will completely collapse. Closing the high seas to fishing is about 60 percent of the oceans. This would benefit all countries. The catch would improve so it would make it that the fish stocks are healthier and therefore larger catch."[23]

While he is concerned about the current destruction of the fish stocks, his work and the work of many scientists has led to great changes.

"Large marine preserves is an idea whose time has come. There are certain areas like Antarctica that could be declared as a marine reserve. Closing the high seas would help large fish like tuna and others. Technically it would work. Coastal fish would not be protected. Species like rock fish would not have protection."[24]

These coastal fish could be protected by local marine reserves and laws of individual nations that have a vested interest in the preservation of their fisheries. The Florida Keys and the recent protection of Bristol Bay are prime examples of the United States working to protect marine wildlife.

The United States must lead on this issue to move the world in the right direction. As Dr. Pauly observed: "The task in the United States is to get the U.S. to ratify the Law of the Seas. It is simply not ratified. The crazies in Congress will not allow it to be ratified."[25]

The collapse of the fisheries is a tragedy of the commons. Since the tuna and other ocean catch belong to everyone they are protected by no one. The goal is to get yours before they are all fished out. By creating a Global High Seas Marine Preserve and inviting all of the fishing nations we can preserve the fish stocks. The 200 mile state limit will insure that nations can still fish. But by protecting the wild stocks out in the high seas they won't be overfished. The tragedy of the commons has resulted in the collapse of the fish stocks. The large fish will be slaughtered to extinction without global protection.

In 1968 Garrett Hardin concluded "a finite world can support only a finite population; therefore, population growth must eventually equal zero". His article in Science "The Tragedy of the Commons" shaped environmental thinking and is required reading to fully understand the problem of the collapse of the fisheries.[26] The tragedy of the commons is the concept that individuals acting independently with their self interest in mind will behave contrary to the best interests of the whole group by depleting some common resource. Here the common resource is the fish that are owned by everyone. Since no one fishing company owns them and no one nation can protect them this resource is over fished. The fishermen try to get their share before every last fish is gone. Despite the limits recommended by scientists without enforcement, the fish stocks continue to decline.

The tragedy of the commons with the fish stocks can be overcome by recognizing that the fisherman cannot be marginalized, but they cannot be subsidized either. The 200 mile national limit will still allow fishing within the national boundaries of the various nations that boarder the oceans. Numerous nations are doing a very good job of creating marine preserves. Now humans just need to take it to the next level and make the high seas off limits to commercial fishing. This legal move will save the fisheries for future generations. The next president needs to call for an international conference for the creation of a Global High Seas Marine Preserve. This political move will get all of the participants together to solve this problem of overfishing.

The U.S. Navy and other navies can enforce the ban on commercial fishing. The United Nations, which many scholars consider toothless, can working through the Security Council oversea this ban. The Law of the Seas Convention has to be amended to create this Global High Seas Marine Preserve. Like all international agreements, it can be accomplished because it is in everyone's interests that the fish humans depend on for food not become extinct.

We have been fishing for thousands of years. We can continue to fish for thousands more. We just cannot empty out the oceans with these giant commercial fishing vessels that make up a very small part of global fishing but do the most damage. The interests of a tiny handful of rich people who are destroying the oceans with commercial fishing are outweighed by humanity's interest in preserving the fish stocks. This is one fight against a handful of wealthy individuals we can win.

---

1 "Global Ocean Legacy - Pew Trusts." Global Ocean Legacy - Pew Trusts.

Accessed July 24, 2015. http://www.pewtrusts.org/en/projects/global-ocean-legacy.

2 "About the National Marine Sanctuaries." About the National Marine Sanctuaries. Accessed July 24, 2015. http://sanctuaries.noaa.gov/about/welcome.html.

3 "MPAtlas » Explore." MPAtlas » Explore. Accessed July 24, 2015. http://www.mpatlas.org/explore/.

4 "About the National Marine Sanctuaries." About the National Marine Sanctuaries. Accessed July 24, 2015. http://sanctuaries.noaa.gov/about/welcome.html.

5 CNN. Accessed July 24, 2015. http://edition.cnn.com/2008/WORLD/asiapcf/03/24/eco.aboutfishing/.

6 "Yahoo Finance - Business Finance." Yahoo Finance. Accessed July 24, 2015. http://finance.yahoo.com/;_ylt=AsD8ugzcr45AhNB5Zdlo3DiHH8V_;_ylu=X3oDMTFkM3NoNmh1BHBvcwMxBHNlYwN5ZmlOYXZUb3BuYXZMZWdvdTmV3BHNsawNmaW5hbmNlaG9tZQ--.

7 Pauly, Daniel. "Aquacalypse Now." Aquacalypse Now. September 28, 2009. Accessed July 24, 2015. http://www.newrepublic.com/article/environment-energy/aquacalypse-now.

8 "Marine Conservation Organizations." Marine Conservation Organizations. Accessed July 24, 2015. http://marinebio.org/oceans/conservation/organizations/index.aspx.

9 Clover, Charles. "Britishseafishing.co.uk." Britishseafishingcouk. Accessed July 24, 2015. http://britishseafishing.co.uk/atlantic-dawn-the-ship-from-hell/.

10 Scherer, Glenn. "Christian-right Views Are Swaying Politicians and Threatening the Environment." Grist. October 27, 2004. Accessed July 24, 2015. http://grist.org/article/scherer-christian/?source=daily.

11 Rosenblum, Mort, and Mar Cabra. "In Mackerel's Plunder, Hints of Epic Fish Collapse." The New York Times. January 24, 2012. Accessed July 25, 2015. http://www.nytimes.com/2012/01/25/science/earth/in-mackerels-plunder-hints-of-epic-fish-collapse.html?_r=0.

12 "FAO Fisheries & Aquaculture - Global Statistical Collections." FAO Fisheries & Aquaculture - Global Statistical Collections. Accessed July 25, 2015. http://www.fao.org/fishery/statistics/en., "Fisheries Latest Data."

Scientific Facts on. Accessed July 25, 2015. http://www.greenfacts.org/en/fisheries/index.htm. And U.S. Census Bureau, "United States Census Bureau." International Programs. Accessed July 25, 2015. http://www.census.gov/ipc/www/worldpop.html.

13 "Fishing & Aquaculture." World Fish Stocks, Fisheries Maps, Aquaculture Statistics. Accessed July 25, 2015. http://www.theglobaleducation-project.org/earth/fisheries-and-aquaculture.php.

14 "Convention on Fishing and Conservation of the Living Resources of the High Seas." Wikipedia. Accessed July 25, 2015. http://en.wikipedia.org/wiki/Convention_on_Fishing_and_Conservation_of_the_Living_Resources_of_the_High_Seas.

15 Howard, Brian Clark. "U.S. Creates Largest Protected Area in the World, 3X Larger Than California." National Geographic. September 26, 2014. Accessed July 25, 2015. http://news.nationalgeographic.com/news/2014/09/140924-pacific-remote-islands-marine-monument-expansion-conservation/. and Galbraith, Kate. "Obama's Ocean Gambit." Foreign Policy Obamas Ocean Gambit Comments. October 10, 2014. Accessed July 25, 2015. http://foreignpolicy.com/2014/10/10/obamas-ocean-gambit/.

16 "North American Free Trade Agreement." Wikipedia. Accessed July 25, 2015. http://en.wikipedia.org/wiki/North_American_Free_Trade_Agreement.

17 "European Union." Wikipedia. Accessed July 25, 2015. http://en.wikipedia.org/wiki/European_Union.

18 *World Ocean Review*. Hamburg: Maribus, 2010.

19 Raab, Lauren. "Island of Kiribati Bans Commercial Fishing in Part of Pacific." Los Angeles Times. June 17, 2014. Accessed July 25, 2015. http://www.latimes.com/science/sciencenow/la-sci-sn-fishing-ban-pacific-kiribati-20140617-story.html.

20 "Interview with Dr. Daniel Pauly." Interview by Danny Quintana. January 13, 2015.

21- 25 Ibid

26. Hardin, Garrrett. "The Tragedy of the Commons." *The Tragedy of the Commons*. Science Magazine, 13 Dec. 1968. Web. 30 July 2015.

CHAPTER 8

Planets, Oceans and Defense Contractors

> "We set sail on this new sea because there is
> new knowledge to be gained and new rights
> to be won, and they must be won and used for
> the progress of all people. For space science,
> like nuclear science and all technology, has no
> conscience of its own. Whether it will become
> a force for good or ill depends on man."
> — PRESIDENT JOHN F. KENNEDY
> AT RICE UNIVERSITY,
> HOUSTON, TEXAS, SEPT. 12, 1962

We are willing to spend hundreds of billions of dollars on a failed "war on drugs" and a failing "war on terror". We are not willing to spend serious money on space and ocean exploration. The political connection is not there to push forward this important change in policy. Instead, we build prisons and the wrong weapons systems for this century. Drug use continues and terrorism becomes worse.

Our country's defense contractors can build anything. They do not want to blow up the world. The executives of these large public companies want what other executives of public companies want: to increase revenue growth and market share. A major world war with millions of global casualties will not help any of these companies. It is not a bad thing that investors and public companies want to make money. This keeps people employed, goods and services circulating and economic activity humming. The top 100 defense contractors enjoy the benefits of an expanding market called the War on Terror. The money flow is heavy.

As long as the War on Terror continues, defense spending will feed the thousands of communities with jobs. Unfortunately, this war on religious criminals will continue for the foreseeable future. These barbarians must be stopped to prevent the collapse of civilization.

Ancient Rome failed to stop the barbarian hordes and the result was a complete disaster for the Western world. Western civilization fell into an abyss. This must not happen again. This time civilization might not rise up from the ruins. Defense spending globally as well as international police work and cooperation to defeat the Taliban, ISIS, Boko Haram and international drug cartels must continue until these dangerous criminals are defeated. We have no choice but to fight back. Criminals must be stopped so everyone can live in peace. Humanity's fate need not be that of ancient Rome, which fell to the criminals of that era. Since dirty, hairy, illiterate, ignorant, smelly barbarians did not care about bathing or sanitation, they destroyed the great aqueducts of ancient Rome.

The dirty, hairy, illiterate, ignorant, smelly members of Al Qaeda, the Taliban, Boko Haram and ISIS don't care what they destroy. Thus museums, works of art, culture and civilization are blown to pieces, stolen or sold off despite the loss to humanity. These criminals use modern technology and weapons to commit horrific crimes. They use cell phones, computers and social media to spread their messages of hate. They want the benefits of modern life and civilization that come with the rule of law but they do not want the responsibilities that come with being good citizens.

With trials come exposure of their crimes and the damage to their victims. If the United States can lock up over 2 million people in a failed "war on drugs," the planet can capture, put on trial and punish the hundreds of thousands of criminals who hide behind religion. The international drug cartels at least don't hide behind the moral mask of religion to justify their crimes.

The Mexican drug cartels are more than willing to kill anyone who opposes them. There is a war going on next door to the United States and it does not get airtime on major media. Over 100,000 Mexicans have been killed in this war and everyday more die from the drug cartel violence. These criminals will only be defeated with prosecutions, fair trials, incarceration.[1] Every time someone in the United States or the European

Union uses cocaine, heroin or meth, someone in a poor country controlled by drug cartels dies.

Defeating these international criminals is a matter of global police and detective work. When religious criminals blew up a French newspaper office, France did not send in the marines or launch a missile strike from a French Mirage fighter. They gathered the evidence, traced the clues and made arrests. Then the individuals who committed this crime were put on trial. If convicted, the applicable legal penalties are imposed, including execution. The "war on terror" like the "war on drugs" needs to be dealt with for what it is, a international legal problem where the rules of civilization are enforced.

Just as the "war on drugs" has failed to stop people from using illegal drugs, the "war on terror" has not stopped religious criminals from robbing, killing, stealing, raping, and kidnapping. Criminals hiding behind religion continue to cause havoc until they are arrested or killed. Both policies have failed and need to be re-examined by the next administration working closely with the European Union, Russia, Japan, China, Latin America, African countries, India and all governments who want law instead of chaos. These criminal organizations are not recognized by any legitimate government.

If you want to see where your tax dollars are going, the following list of major contractors gives you an idea of what battling terrorists unsuccessfully costs. But this is just the financial part. Not included is the human cost of what alternative spending would do for society.

Top 20 defense contractors, 2014

By Defense Systems Staff Jul 15, 2014

The U.S. defense budget continues a downward trend after the wars in Iraq and Afghanistan. The Obama administration's $495.6 budget request for 2015 was the first in 13 years not predicated on U.S. troops being involved in a foreign war and accounts for a reduction in the size of U.S. forces.

But defense still accounts for a sizable chunk of federal spending, making up 55 percent of the 2015 request. Below are the top 20 defense contractors for 2014, based on revenue from prime contracts during fiscal 2013.

Rank	Top Defense Companies	Defense Revenue ($ Millions – Fiscal 2013)
1	Lockheed Martin Corp.	$10,402
2	Northrop Grumman Corp.	$5,873
3	Raytheon Co.	$5,016
4	Boeing Co.	$3,585
5	General Dynamics Corp.	$3,150
6	Hewlett Packard Co.	$2,593
7	DynCorp International Llc	$2,485
8	Leidos Inc.	$2,426
9	Booz Allen Hamilton	$2,126
10	Fluor Corp.	$2,079
11	L-3 Communications Corp.	$1,600
12	ManTech International Corp.	$1,501
13	CACI International Inc.	$1,491

14	Computer Sciences Corp.	$1,426
15	Exelis Inc.	$1,350
16	BAE Systems Inc.	$1,255
17	Harris Corp.	$1,221
18	Science Applications International Corp.	$1,155
19	United Technologies Corp.	$962
20	Jacobs Engineering Group Inc.	$837

Source: Washington Technology[2]

These companies are multi-market business enterprises that can engage in a host of business activities. Lockheed Martin is a prime example. In addition to being the premier defense contractor on the planet, they also make products for space exploration. In their own words:

> Lockheed Martin Corporation is a customer-focused, global enterprise principally engaged in the research, design, development, manufacture and integration of advanced technology systems, products and services for government and commercial customers. The Corporation's core business areas are systems integration, aeronautics, space and technology services.[3]

Lockheed is one of NASA's largest contractors. At times they will team up with other major defense contractors to accomplish incredible projects, like the Space Shuttle.

Human Exploration and Development of Space: Since the first Shuttle flight in 1981, Lockheed Martin has supplied NASA with the External Tank which holds fuel for the orbiter's main engines.[4]

The Boeing Corporation manufactures planes for our airlines and those of various companies worldwide. The company also produces missiles for our strategic weapons program and manufacture giant rocket engines that took men to the moon.[5]

Northrop Grumman owns Newport News Shipbuilding. It describes itself:

Northrop Grumman Newport News builds and maintains the most sophisticated ships in the world – nuclear powered aircraft carriers and submarines. [6]

Only a handful of nations possess aircraft carriers. These nations are primarily from Western Europe. Even India with a population of approximately 1.1 billion has an aircraft carrier. Brazil and Argentina have aircraft carriers.[7] These are horrendously expensive pieces of equipment. The total life cycle cost of a Nimitz-class aircraft approximately is $22 billion dollars.[8] This is for just one carrier. We have a fleet of 10 carriers to project our military power anywhere in the world.[9]

The Reagan administration initiated the largest military build-up in history. This 600 ship Navy with 10 aircraft carriers was not without cost. In the eight years he was in office, the Democrats and Republicans spent so much money on defense they converted the largest creditor nation on Earth to the largest debtor.[10]

What will it cost to explore the oceans? Certainly it will be less than the price of one aircraft carrier or one nuclear submarine. The problem with deep-sea exploration is it is very difficult. Ocean pressure increases with depth. If this was easy, the remaining 95 percent of the unexplored oceans would already be explored. Since Newport News is in the shipbuilding business and has tremendous expertise, as do their competitors, it only makes sense to have Congress fund a deep sea exploration program.

Our nuclear submarines are the best in the world. The Virginia Class submarines:

"......are the most advanced submarines in the world

.....will maintain the nation's undersea supremacy well into the 21st century

.....have a crew complement of 100 sailors and officers

.....can stay submerged for periods of up to 3 months at a time.[11]

These submarines are the best weapon systems in their class in human history. One submarine armed with nuclear missiles can destroy 200 cities.[13] But they have almost no capability for deep sea exploration. It is not that we cannot build a very large submarine for this purpose. Newport News is a world-class ship builder and can design and build any type of sea vessel. It is just that Congress has not commissioned the exploration of the oceans as a high priority item. The leadership is not there to initiate this program.

Exploration of the inner solar system languishes due to the same lack of political leadership. The last time a man was on the moon was over 30 years ago. After we reached the moon and failed to strike gold or oil, we gave up on further exploration. You need volcanic activity for gold and vegetation for oil and the moon fails on both counts. Other worlds within our own solar system probably do not have oil. Europa has volcanic activity and some of the larger planets like Jupiter and Neptune appear to be composed of various gases. The asteroid belt probably has valuable minerals.

It is not that we cannot build spacecraft for exploration of the inner solar system; again Congress has failed in providing leadership. Lockheed Martin, Raytheon, Northrop Grumman and the various other defense contractors have armies of engineers and lobbyists looking for projects that will continue their careers and enrich their company's coffers.

In awarding the largest defense contract in history — more than $200 billion dollars — Congress and the Bush administration committed the United States to building the controversial Joint Strike Fighter.[13] Whether the nation needs this fighter plane is not an issue. How a plane of this type will stop a criminal religious zealot with a stick of dynamite strapped to some radioactive hospital waste is also a mystery.

And if this very expensive piece of hardware was not enough, Lockheed Martin is also the contractor for the F/A 22 Raptor. This is an amazing piece of hardware. The capabilities of this combat aircraft are truly a technological marvel.

In Lockheed Martin's own words:

The F/A-22 Raptor is a new breed of super-fighter for the 21st century. With its stealth, supersonic cruise, agility and advanced integrated avionics, it will dominate the skies over any future battlefield and bring unequaled capability into the hands of America's Air Force fighter pilots.[14]

The problem again is the employees of Lockheed Martin do not want to lose their jobs. Nobody wants to be unemployed. If the choice is cutting the defense budget and more unemployment or building a fighter plane that adds absolutely nothing to the nation's security, Congress is going to borrow and spend more money on defense.

Lockheed Martin, Boeing, Raytheon and the various other air force contractors can land men on the moon and/or build the necessary vehicles to take men or robots to Mars or beyond. They can build the ships for exploring the inner solar system. But Congress cannot see the wisdom of starting a program that extends beyond their next election.

1 "Mexican Drug War."Wikipedia. Accessed July 25, 2015. http://en.wikipedia.org/wiki/Mexican_Drug_War.

2 Top 20 Defense Contractors. http://www.your-poc.com/top-20-defense-contractors-2015/."Top 100 Defense Contractors." Government Executive. August 15, 2009. Accessed July 25, 2015. http://www.govexec.com/features/0809-15/0809-15s3s1.htm.

3 "Sustainability." Lockheed Martin · Lockheed Martin. Accessed July 25, 2015. http://www.lockheedmartin.com/.

4 Ibid

5 "Remembering "The Highway Of Death" By Malcom Lagauche." Remembering "The Highway Of Death" By Malcom Lagauche. Accessed July 25, 2015. http://www.countercurrents.org/lagauche280210.htm.

6 "Newport News Shipbuilding." Newport News Shipbuilding. Accessed July 25, 2015. http://www.nns.com/.

7 Toppan, Andrew. "World's Aircraft Carriers." November 26, 2001. http%3A%2F%2Fwww.hazegray.org%2Fnavhist%2Fcarriers%2Fsummary.htm.

8 "CVN-68 Nimitz-class." - Navy Ships. Accessed July 25, 2015. http://www.fas.org/man/dod-101/sys/ship/cvn-68.htm.

9 Ibid, at: http://www.fas.org/man/dod-101/sys/ship/index.html

10 Greider, William. "Debtor Nation."The Nation. April 22, 2004. Accessed July 25, 2015. http://www.thenation.com/article/debtor-nation/.

11 "Submarines - Newport News Shipbuilding." Submarines - Newport News Shipbuilding. Accessed July 25, 2015. http://nns.huntingtoningalls.com/products/subs/index.

12 "CVN-68 Nimitz-class." - Navy Ships. Accessed July 25, 2015. http://www.fas.org/man/dod-101/sys/ship/cvn-68.htm.

13 "Sustainability." Lockheed Martin · Lockheed Martin. Accessed July 25, 2015. http://www.lockheedmartin.com/.

14 Ibid at: http://www.lockheedmartin.com/factsheets/product2.html

CHAPTER 9

The Benefits of Space and Ocean Exploration

> A rat done bit my sister Nell with whitey on
> the moon her face and arms began to swell and
> whitey is on the moon I can't pay no doctor
> bills but whitey is on the moon ten years from
> now I'll be payin' still with whitey on the
> moon ya know? the man just upped my rent
> last night cause whitey is on the moon no hot
> water no toilets no lights but whitey is on the
> moon I wonder why he's uppin' me? cause
> whitey is on the moon well I was givin' him 50
> dollars a week and now whitey is on the moon
> — JOHN COLTRANE
> "WHITEY ON THE MOON

During the Age of Discovery, Spain, Portugal, France, Holland and England explored, developed overseas colonies and their economies prospered. The stay-at-home nations of China, Japan, Germany, Turkey, Russia and Italy were temporarily left behind by history. The non-explorer societies missed out on important opportunities. By the time these other European and Asian powers caught up and developed their navies, Spain and Great Britain were well on the way toward domination of the oceans. Almost 300 years and numerous wars later, by the 1800s, the sun never set on the British Empire.[1]

The United States has developed a space program that surpassed the initial successes of the former Soviet Union. Today there is indecision and questions about our country's will to go forward into the frontiers of outer space. The failure of a second space shuttle has given politicians and critics of NASA the opportunity to question public spending on space exploration. Clearly space exploration is perceived as very expensive with little return. This perception is misguided.

Many benefits have come from space exploration. The technological spin-offs have been numerous and diverse. We have much better medicine and medical devices as a direct result of the research necessary to make the short journey to space successful.

Today we measure blood pressure instantly as a result of the Mercury scientists' need to protect Alan Shepard during blast off.[2] We have scratch-resistant lens for eye glasses as a result of NASA's need to protect satellites from space debris.[4] Braces for teeth fit easier as a result of Nitinol, an alloy used to make satellite deployment easier.[5] Electronic pain-control devices implanted in patients were born from space program telemetry.[6] The patient can control the pain as a result of the miniature electronic components developed from the space program.[7] Heart pacemakers developed in part from the electronic monitoring used to operate satellites in earth orbit.[8] The implantable insulin pump borrowed technology from the robot arm on the first Mars Voyager probe.[9]

The view from space has resulted in tremendous new knowledge about the Earth below. We have topography maps that have made navigation easier and safer and we have developed new sciences. Virtually all of us use Google Earth and maps daily.

From studies on the greenhouse gases that affect global climate change to assisting archaeologists with burial sites, scientific observations and mapping of the rain forests, space exploration has been tremendously useful in expanding the boundaries of human knowledge. Obviously, weather and communications satellites have made our lives more comfortable and the world a smaller place. The result is we can talk by phone to our loved ones on the other side of the planet on vacation in Bali, Indonesia, or get their flight schedule while they wait to board an airline in Sydney, Australia. We can use video-conference technology to communicate with friends and family thousands of miles apart. We can ask our phones for driving directions to get to a public gathering. All of these benefits are the spinoffs from space exploration.

Some scholars argue that exploration is a natural event that is an intricate part of human existence. Exploration is best explained in the social sciences and not as a list of business and medical benefits that naturally flow from discovery. Some scholars have argued that the failure to continue with human exploration would lead to the demise of human civilization. Today our world view is different from that of people who lived in the 1800s. We can actually picture the Earth and most of us see the planet as a small globe in a sea of darkness, we have become so familiar with the images from the various shuttle missions to outer space.

Humans are the frustrated, aggressive animal. We have perfected the art of war and practice of killing. Left on this planet to our own devices, we will completely destroy the Earth and all of God's creation. What re-directing the immense human energy away from the planet toward outer space will accomplish is we will be less inclined to commit total and complete genocide of all living things. We use war as an instrument of policy to carry out politics regardless of the wishes of the mass of humanity.

Space exploration is more difficult than anything we have ever tried to accomplish in all of our previous ventures into the unknown. While there are not space monsters that will swallow up our space ships, there will be very real dangers of which we are well aware. When Europeans ventured forth to colonize following the explorers who had gone before them, the difficult part had already taken place. Colonization followed exploration.

We are frightened away from building a moon base and landing on Mars not because we can't, but because it is exceptionally difficult and we know it. We have the technology but we know there are not rivers leading to exotic tropical paradise with waterfalls and pools full of fish surrounded by lush green plants. The moon is a barren rock devoid of all life and of questionable mineral value. The criticism that it is difficult to justify spending the billions of dollars required to develop a moon base when the money could be better spent on Earth is not accurate.

All of the money for space exploration is spent here on Earth. All of the hardware, infrastructure, resources and science to build these facilities take place on land. What goes into space is the finished product. The end result is the spaceship just as the car that leaves the factory is what was bought and driven. The factory itself does not go anywhere but continues to employ workers and generate jobs and economic activity.

The reality is money is not better spent on other defense projects. We waste hundreds of billions of dollars on weapons systems of questionable utility and keep bases open that are politically connected. Building a moon base will refine many of the medical, computer and propulsion technologies and make our journeys to the inner solar system easier. Just having such powerful militaries makes their use tempting to carry out goals of politics through war. If the United States did not have the ability to invade another country in violation of international law, we would not do it.

Instead of invading countries in this century the better approach is to incorporate these developing economies into a much larger international space program. There are several benefits which will have long-term positive impact on humanity. The technology transfer will accelerate economic development in the belt near the equator where current immigration pressures exist. Workers with good jobs and stable societies don't emigrate.

As I was flying to Portugal after a wheelchair distribution to the island nation of Sao Tome where my Portuguese ancestors processed slaves before shipping them to Brazil and the Caribbean, I was amazed. I was flying at 37,000 feet above the earth where my ancestors were on these flimsy little wooden ships braving the unknown. My flight home was five hours late. The island is still as beautiful as when my ancestors first discovered it. Now it is crowded with over 200,000 people. There is a modern airport, roads, electricity and the Internet. The U.S. Navy painted the schools and built a security fence for the airport.

Had my Portuguese and Spanish ancestors not been brave, would I by flying in this Airbus above the earth looking down at these land areas where we all might have different skin color but are all God's children? Would America be America if our ancestors were not brave enough to venture forth into the unknown? Would we have international jet travel? What would life be like if people stopped being brave and just gave up on exploration 500 years ago?

By slowly shifting defense spending to space exploration using the same contractors and congressional districts, we can keep people employed nationally and get the benefits that will come about from the push forward with discovery. Our present defense budget cannot be cut because it is easy political spending but ineffective in solving global environmental problems.

Freezing the defense budget at its current level and giving the mission of ocean and space exploration to the Department of Defense will enable the aerospace contractors and navy contractors to continue to employ people and protect our international interests. These programs of building a sustainable space station, a moon base and a manned mission to Mars are not that expensive when compared to total consumer spending and other budget items. Can you imagine how much it will cost humanity if we have a global war between Islam and the West, as is the goal of ISIS? Then exploring the oceans and Mars looks rather cheap.

This change in direction from the military-industrial complex to a space-ocean-exploration-development complex can be accomplished as follows: If the United States re-directs defense spending by ten percent annually toward space and ocean exploration, in five years we can demilitarize the economy and create millions of jobs. The United States will still have the largest defense budget on the planet. It will also have entire new and much-needed industries that will give young people hope of great employment and adventure.

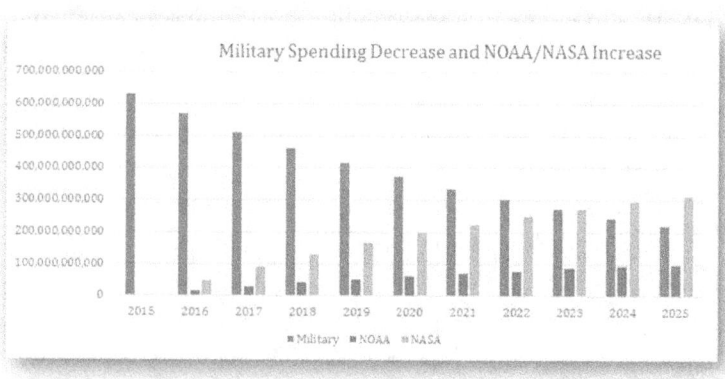

Chart by Aaron Crabtree

We owe it to future generations that they will have a planet where the fish stocks have not become extinct and exciting employment opportunities exist. Humanity needs a change of direction from massive defense spending building the weapons of the last century. Change will occur. We can react to events or have the foresight of Thomas Jefferson and look far into the future. All that is required is courage and vision.

Public attitudes toward space exploration have changed. Vladimir Surdin, senior fellow at the Sternberg State Astronomical Institute observes:

> "Most people in developed countries no longer feel the same patriotic excitement over manned space flights that people used to feel in 1960s and 1970s, with the possible exception of China. Today, being a cosmonaut is an extreme and dangerous profession. It is similar to being a soldier, test pilot, deep-sea submersible pilot, mountain climber and so on. The overall trend in all these professions is to keep people out of danger. Submersible robots and unmanned aerial vehicles, tanks and military machines - they are cheaper and more reliable, "[10]

According to Surdin, human beings cannot compete with robots in space. For example, NASA's Mars rover, Opportunity, has been on the red planet for seven years already. The robotic spacecraft Odyssey has been orbiting the planet for a decade, and Voyager spacecraft have been in use for more than three decades. "The data-to-cost ratio of these spacecraft is hundreds of times greater than that of manned space missions," the scientist noted. The effects of space conditions on the human body have been thoroughly studied over the past 50 years, leading Surdin to ask: "Why continue spending huge amounts of money looking into minor details if it is already clear that a manned flight to the Moon is possible while a manned flight to Mars is almost impossible?"[11]

The environmental and economic problems facing mankind are beyond the scope of any political party. These are human issues that need to be addressed by all democracies in all elections. As humans we have more in common than our limited religious and political differences. We all have a shared interest in survival.

1 "British Empire: Introduction." British Empire: Introduction. Accessed July 25, 2015. http://www.britishempire.co.uk/intro/intro.htm.

2 Rutz, Dan. "From pace Makers to Braces, the Medical Benefits of Space Exploration." CNN. November 2, 1998. Accessed July 25, 2015. http://www.cnn.com/HEALTH/9811/02/space.medical/.

3 to 9. Ibid

9 NASA. "HSF." Science and Technology Applications. Accessed July 25, 2015. http://www.spaceflight.nasa.gov/shuttle/benefits/srtm_benefits.html.

10 http://www.spacedaily.com/reports/The_Benefits_Of_Space_Exploration_999.html.

11 Ibid.

CHAPTER 10

New Kids on the Block

> "We choose to go to the moon in this decade and do the other things, not because they are easy, but because they are hard, because that goal will serve to organize and measure the best of our energies and skills, because that challenge is one that we are willing to accept, one we are unwilling to postpone, and one which we intend to win."
> — PRESIDENT JOHN F. KENNEDY

There is one clear advantage a modern capitalist system has over other economic systems: innovation. We create more new inventions, file more patents, develop more entire new markets than any society in human history. New markets are created with risk. Entrepreneurial genius Steve Jobs pushed the limits of new frontiers with Apple Computer and the smartphone, iPod and the changes that resulted in consumer habits. Now billions of people are tied to the Internet with their phones and computers. The world today is completely unlike that of our grandparents. In many areas it is just better. We use indoor toilets, take hot showers, watch flat-screen televisions, have incredible music available and access world-class medical care — provided we live in a developed country in the European Union or the United States and Canada.

Certainly our planet has more people than ever before. The upside of more people and a larger gene pool is there are more talented individuals like Steve Jobs, Elon Musk, James Cameron, Paul Allen, Bill Gates, Olga Kern, Neil deGrasse Tyson and millions of others. There is also incredible technology. The downside is there are over 7 billion people. There is no one religious book or scientific manual or political or economic plan for humanity. Human society is like a car traveling at maximum speed with no lights on, no driver and no idea where we are going. In the United States the nearest we come to a social plan is the ethos is consumption. What's next for humanity and the planet? Is a third and final attempt at mass suicide that will bring about the "end of times" and the "apocalypse" humanity's fate? The future is unknown. But there are some very intelligent people who think humanity and life on the planet has a future.

Steve Jobs has passed on but other very bright men and women have picked up his mantle of creativity. There are some very exciting companies out there pursuing the new frontiers of space and ocean exploration. SpaceX has a man of equal genius, Elon Musk. Their goal is ambitious. In their words, "SpaceX designs, manufactures and launches advanced rockets and spacecraft. The company was founded in 2002 to revolutionize space technology, with the ultimate goal of enabling people to live on other planets."[1] With over 3,000 employees and growing, Dr. Musk understands that making space flight affordable will require creating reusable vehicles. His hope is to bring down the cost of taking objects to outer space to $10 per pound.[2]

Space X has made substantial breakthroughs in almost every area of lowering costs. The space shuttle was very expensive. "We've made substantial breakthroughs in the design of the structure, the avionics, the engines and the launch operations."

"We view our primary competitors in the long term as China in particularity and Russia and there is no enforceability of patents against those countries."[3] His company is already profitable. He sees Mars as the only realistic option for human exploration. He looks at having a fully reusable rocket system, "then you are just down to the cost of the propellant." He seeks to make space travel to Mars at a cost of $500,000 per person. "Could a middle-class person sell all of their stuff and move to Mars if they wanted to? I think that is the threshold for making human life interplanetary." He is confident that price can be achieved in the long term. Given his successes with PayPal, SolarCity, Tesla and the need to reduce costs for space travel, I would not bet against him. He thinks it can be done within ten years. His firm is hiring engineers. Mars can be done and he believes "we can eventually make Mars like Earth"[4]. This company is exciting.

"I think the most important thing is to preserve the future of humanity and that we have done everything we can to insure that human civilization will last as long as possible. I think that is the sensible thing to do and the longer we last the more we will learn and the more we will discover. I am most concerned about insuring the longevity of humanity. I think there are some people out there who seem as though they don't like humanity and that humans are a blight on the surface of the earth and certainly humanity has done some terrible things. I think on

balance humanity has done some wonderful things, I personally love humanity and we should attempt to do everything to
preserve life as we know it."[5]

NASA is his biggest customer. "I think there is always going
to be a very important role for NASA and other space agencies
around the world. Space exploration will always be a govern-
ment-private joint endeavor, I think. I think over time it will be
majority private but government will always have a significant
role to play as it does in the rest of the economy.[6]"

Mr. Musk is not the only successful entrepreneur with
space ambitions. Jeff Bezos of Amazon fame from an early age
has been interested in space exploration and tourism as well as
planetary defense from asteroids. His company Blue Origin has
done impressive work on reusable launch vehicles. Now they
are teaming up with other companies and winning contracts
from NASA and the U.S. Air Force.

> "A profile published in 2013 described a 1982 Miami
> Herald interview Bezos gave after he was named vale-
> dictorian of his high school class. The 18-year-old
> Bezos "said he wanted to build space hotels, amuse-
> ment parks and colonies for 2 million or 3 million
> people who would be in orbit. 'The whole idea is to
> preserve the earth,' he told the newspaper .... The goal
> was to be able to evacuate humans. The planet would
> become a park."[7]

Humanity will survive as a result of the efforts of Elon Musk,
Richard Brandson and Paul Allen, Robert Bigelow, Jeff Bezos
and others. These pioneers see the much larger picture. It is not

just space tourism and launch services that these individuals are seeking to achieve with their commercial ventures. They have plenty of money. A billionaire can spend over $1 million per year for 1,000 years and not run out of money. These concerned individuals are out to save the planet from complete destruction. *What they are pursuing is a new direction for mankind.*

They understand that if humanity is to survive, we MUST explore the inner solar system and preserve the fish stocks. They are pioneers in their fields, not politicians who set public policy. The combined value of all of the private companies engaged in space exploration does not even come close to the cost of the missile defense system, at over $250 billion[8]. The joint strike fighter program costs over $396 billion and the operational costs are even higher.[9]

Criticism leveled at them that their space exploration efforts are being pursued for ego is misguided. See "The Billionaire Space Club" by Charles Seife:

"It's an old trick. Multimillionaires regularly try to spin acts of crass ego gratification as selfless philanthropy, no matter how obviously self-serving. They jump out of balloons at the edge of the atmosphere, take submarines to the bottom of the ocean, or shoot endangered animals on safari, all in the name of science and exploration. The more recent trend is billionaires making fleets of rocket ships for private space exploration. What makes this one different is that the public actually seems to buy the farce. Space buffs everywhere are acting as if everyone in the world will somehow be enriched when Lady Gaga is finally able to sip pink

Cristal in zero gravity. Call it the trickle-down theory of space exploration: Somehow, building a luxury-liner suborbital rocket ship for the amusement of the ultrarich, ultrafamous, and ultrabored will be a great victory for all of humanity."[10]

Self-aggrandizement is not why these world-class businessmen want space tourism, to explore Mars and the inner solar system.

Richard Branson, exploring the frontier of megalomania.

Photo illustration by *Slate*. Photos by NASA;
Paul Ellis/AFP/Getty Images

They want the public to become excited again about space exploration. They understand the hard data and want huge changes in global policy. They are trying to save civilization from disaster and a certain collision course with mass extinction of all species.

Elon Musk' vision of Mars colonies is shared by many scientists and space enthusiasts. But despite his immense talent and enthusiasm, it is doubtful that exploration and colonization of Mars can be accomplished by private entrepreneurs. Exploring and eventually colonizing Mars will have to be a global effort involving several nations. This endeavor is too great to be accomplished by private industry. Even billionaires have their limits. Musk's plan for Mars is intriguing but not feasible. According to Space.com:

> "Elon Musk, the billionaire founder and CEO of the private spaceflight company SpaceX, wants to help establish a Mars colony of up to 80,000 people by ferrying explorers to the Red Planet for perhaps $500,000 a trip. In Musk's vision, the ambitious Mars settlement program would start with a pioneering group of fewer than 10 people, who would journey to the Red Planet aboard a huge reusable rocket powered by liquid oxygen and methane. "At Mars, you can start a self-sustaining civilization and grow it into something really big," Musk told an audience at the Royal Aeronautical Society in London on Friday (Nov. 16). Musk was there to talk about his business plans, and to receive the Society's gold medal for his contribution to the commercialization of space.[11]

The cost of a successful trip to Mars will be like every other human adventure. It will be planned by humans and eventually accomplished despite great danger, loss of life and material. The dollar cost has been estimated on the low side at $6 billion to a high side estimate of over $500 billion.[12] One man who has been in the game the longest is Robert Zubrin, founder of the Mars Society. He envisions using materials already on Mars to reduce costs. Dr. Zubrin's life work is pushing forth humanity's exploration of the Red Planet. His classic book, "The Case For Mars" lays out exactly how using existing technology, we can go further than humans have gone before. But O. Glenn Smith, former manager of shuttles systems engineering at NASA's Johnson Space Center, and Paul D. Spudis, staff scientist at the Lunar and Planetary Institute in Houston, critics of human exploration of Mars, estimate the cost of landing humans on Mars at over $1.5 trillion.[13]

Dr. Zubrin' response to critics who say exploring Mars will be too expensive is:

> To get a grasp of how absurd these estimates are, one need only point out that current and recent NASA budgets have been around $18 billion, including a human spaceflight budget of about $4 billion. So what Smith and Spudis are claiming is that sending nine flights to Mars would cost NASA's full budget for the next 80 years, or the entirety of its human spaceflight budget for 375 years.
>
> Nothing of the sort is necessary. Sending humans to Mars does not involve building fantastical, enormous interplanetary spaceships. Rather, it requires three flight elements of about 100 metric tons mass, comprising 30 tons of payload and 70 tons of trans-Mars

propulsion, each of which could be delivered to orbit by two SpaceX Falcon Heavy rockets or one augmented NASA Space Launch System booster."[14]

The reality is there are as many cost estimates on what it will take to land humans on Mars as there are nations, organizations and individuals who are interested in this important endeavor. Different conferences come up with new cost estimates. Technology changes and costs come down as we find new and less expensive ways to achieve our goals. This is normal human progress and technological change. One panel of experts concluded $100 billion and 20 years could get us there. They seek to burst the myth of $1 trillion as the cost of making humans an interplanetary species.

While a two-decade campaign to prepare a manned mission to Mars would certainly be expensive, it would cost nothing close to the $1 trillion figure that has sometimes been cited, the panel concluded. Instead the mission could be funded out of the current NASA budget, with allowances for inflation, along with contributions from other countries.

One of our goals has been to destroy that '$1 trillion to send a human to Mars' myth, and we have," said Chris Carberry, executive director of the nonprofit ExploreMars group. It's feasible, it's affordable, and it can be done without impacting the federal budget or the NASA budget," he said. "This message is getting across, and there's more support now in Congress and the public for [sending] humans to Mars than ever before."[15]

The challenges of a Mars trip are unlike anything humans have ever undertaken. In addition to having to take all life support systems, there is radiation and a long flight without the possibility of rescue if something goes wrong. Every American administration advocates exploration and colonization of Mars. President Obama alluded to Americans landing on Mars by 2030 in his 2015 State of the Union address. The reality of life is the United States cannot afford to pursue a manned mission to Mars given the cost involved and the current state of our space program. It can be done if defense spending is re-directed toward space and ocean exploration. As Marc Kaufman points out in his National Geographic piece on landing humans on Mars:

"Sending astronauts to Mars could be done at a small fraction of the cost of developing and flying the F-35 fighter jet, according to a rough estimate put forward by a panel of NASA, industry, and academic experts. "[16]

Great new companies like SpaceX and Virgin Atlantic will one day have the capability to take humans from lower earth orbit to space hotels. But that is a far stretch from a successful round trip to the hostile Red planet. The Red planet must be explored by robots in the short run, until the transportation systems improve and the time required to get to Mars is reduced dramatically.

The costs of this exploration can be absorbed by several nations working together. Between the United States, Russia, the

European Union, China, Japan, India and Brazil, the resources exist not only to explore Mars but to colonize it. This has to be pursued as a "human" expedition to Mars and beyond. Given the global problems on this planet, a human expedition to Mars will build unity among competitive nations and foster much-needed international cooperation.

What will reduce costs of launches to earth orbit is for space-capable nations and private entrepreneurs to build their launch facilities near the equator. Some of these countries have very good infrastructure and talented work forces like Kigali, Rwanda, and Cuzco, Peru. India has a rocket launch site at the Thumba Equatorial Rocket Launching Station (TERLS). The TERLS launch site is operated by the Indian Space Research Organization. It is located very close to earth's magnetic equator.[17]

Again, the transfer of technology to Africa and South America and the creation of high tech jobs and infrastructure will accomplish several very important human objectives: lower population growth by increasing education, increase economic activity and thereby lessen immigration pressures. Rwanda has an excellent university, improving infrastructure, transparency in government, an intelligent workforce and a stable government. People there are tri-lingual in English, French and Rwandan. Situated being high above sea level and near the equator, this small country is ideally suited for a spaceport. They have a very good international airport and Tanzania next door borders the ocean and has a large port at Dar El Salem. The added advantage for these private space entrepreneurs is their money will go much farther in the developing world. The scientific talent can be developed or, in the case of India, already exists but at far lower costs.

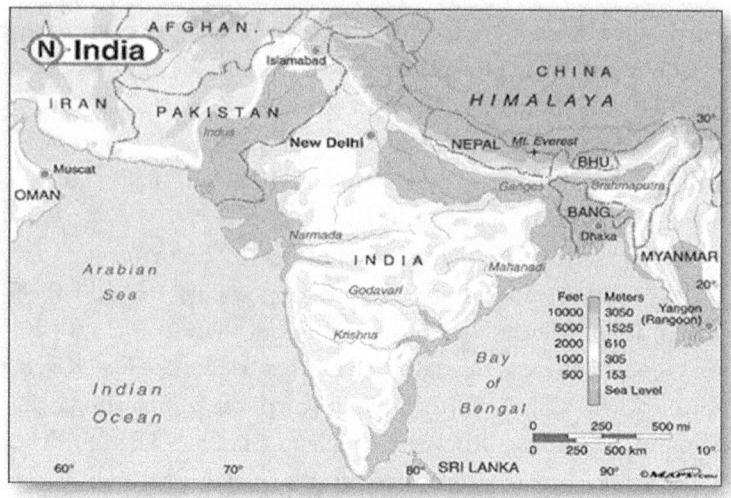

Rwanda is only one of two places on earth where people can safely go on an ecotourism journey and see mountain gorillas. The Rwandan government works very hard to protect these endangered beautiful creatures. The cost of a permit was about $500 when I visited that beautiful country in 2011. The country has amazing beauty and very intelligent people. With their location near the equator and at one of the highest altitudes as well as home to an ambitious work force, this country will soon become the Switzerland of Africa. They are the model on how to overcome genocide and adversity. A spaceport built by private industry with cooperation from NASA, the Russians, Chinese and European as well as the Indian space programs will do wonders in helping technology transfers to a fast-developing Africa. Everyone interested in travel should visit this wonderful country. It is clean, beautiful and the people are very friendly.

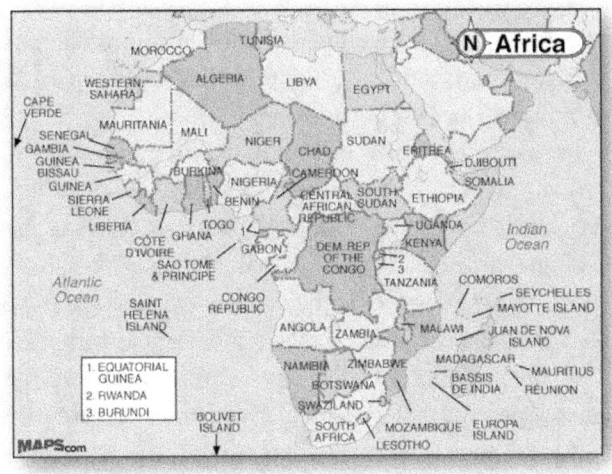

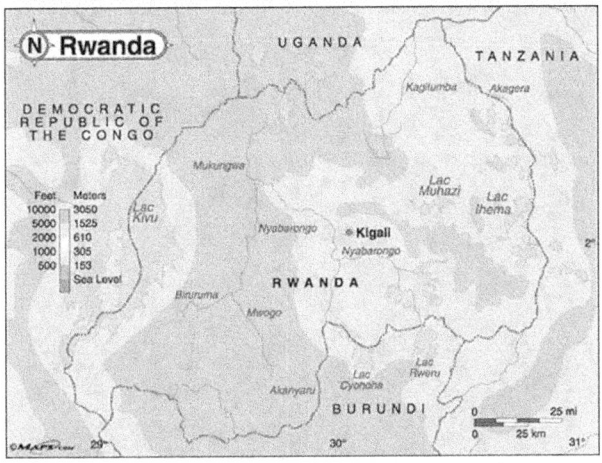

The Incas were among the most highly developed and civilized society in the Americas prior to their destruction by my ruthless Spanish ancestors. Peru's capital city, Cusco, is near the equator but at 10,800 feet. The high altitude, extensive infrastructure, highly developed tourist accommodations and excellent universities make this country ideal for a space launch site in conjunction with Ecuador next door..

In Peru or next door in Quito, Ecuador, sites are ideally suited to launch vehicles into earth orbit. Brazil is next door and their neighbors have an active space program, Agencia Espacial Brasileira. Initially Brazil worked with the United States, but when technology transfers proved difficult, they expanded and worked with Russia, China, India and the Ukraine. Their launch site is the closest of all space ports to the Equator. Brazil became the first Portuguese-speaking nation to partner with the International Space Station. One of their astronauts, Marcos Pontes, was trained in the United States and Russia. He did some scientific experiments for his country and continues to train for his next mission.[18]

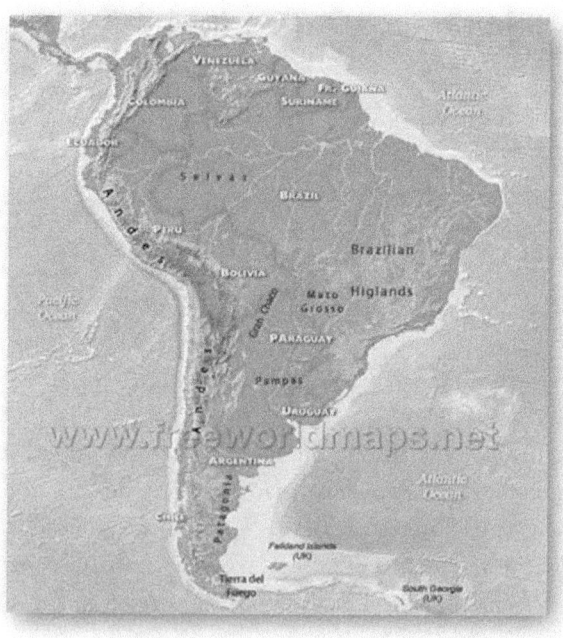

The Europeans have a launch site in French Guiana, the Centre Spatial Guanais. This is a French and European spaceport near Kourou.[19] Its proximity to the Equator makes it particularly suitable for a space port. The spinning of the earth provides extra velocity to the rockets when they are launched eastward.

Japan has an active space program that is built on a lean, shoestring budget and is intimately involved in the peaceful development of space.[20] One of the most technologically advanced nations on the planet, Japan could at any time build nuclear weapons complete with ICBMs. Their astronauts have served missions on the International Space Station. Japan works closely with the United States in launching communication satellites into orbit and their companies provide parts for various space missions. Japan depends on the United States for military protection and works closely with us to keep the peace. As Kate Wilkinson observed in a piece on Asian space exploration:

"Although economic and fiscal hurdles exist, the budget is not the biggest problem. Japan has already developed a world-class space industry on a shoestring. Its estimated official space budget averages less than $4 billion a year, which puts it at roughly half the budget of something like the U.S. National Science Foundation. It is difficult not to be impressed by what the country has achieved thus far. Measure for measure, the development of Japan's space technologies may be among the most, if not the most, efficient in terms of cost-effectiveness. The problem is also not pacifist constitutional constraints that appeared to urge the use of space for exclusively peaceful purposes, as this concept was at last clarified through Japan's Basic Space Law in 2008. The biggest limiting factor for Japan will probably be human capital, as the Japanese cadre of scientists and engineers that constitute the space workforce diminish further in the face of demographic challenges. The estimated space workforce for Japan today is roughly 6,500 workers, in comparison to China's 50,000. One virtue of the small satellite development efforts in Japan is that spreading this work into universities and other institutes helps to cultivate younger engineering and scientific talents."[21]

Iran has a small space program and has successfully launched satellites into orbit. It is one of the founding members of the United Nations Committee on the Peaceful Uses of Outer Space.[22]

Pakistan too is reaching out to the heavens.[23] With a nuclear power India next door, the Pakistanis are working hard to develop their own launch capabilities. North Korea has a variety of rockets and nuclear weapons to protect their hermit kingdom.[24] Will these programs be used to build a better world or will they be used to deliver nuclear explosives to commit genocide?

What is surprising is the level of success some countries have had with space exploration activities. Little know programs like those of Agenzia Spaziale Italiana operated a satellite launch facility off the coast of Kenya at San Marcos Island near the Equator. Italy was one of the founders of the European Space Agency and has worked with NASA on a variety of projects. Italy is ideally suited to expand the technology transfer to

Africa. As suggested earlier, a launch site needs to be developed in central Africa because proximity to the equator is better for lessening the pressures of liftoff to lower earth orbit.[25]

The total budget of all of the world's space programs is quite small, probably less than $60 billion.[26] This is approximately the same amount spent on pet food in the United States, where 40 percent of Americans have at least one dog. Retail giant WalMart has annual revenues of over $480 billion.[27] The U.S. budget for national defense is approximately $1 trillion if you include all relevant programs like the Department of Energy and Veterans Affairs, as well as the related costs of prior wars.[28]

The reality is very little money is spent on space exploration by the United States and other nations. Some spending that involves the use of outer space is hidden from public view because it is contained within other budgets like defense, ocean exploration or other agencies.

What the new kids on the block like Elon Musk can do is expand SpaceX or similar companies and use the resources of the countries near the Equator to lessen their launch load costs to lower earth orbit. Over 52 countries have satellites in outer space and interest in space exploration.[29]

The innovation of small companies and entrepreneurs is probably the best hope for exploration of the cosmos and eventual terra-forming and colonization of Mars. The labor costs in Peru/Ecuador, Rwanda and Kenya, Brazil and Guiana as well as India will make rocketing from the Equator more economically feasible. Brazil and India have the added advantages of existing large manufacturing bases and large scientific and engineering pools.

Elon Musk almost went broke when the U.S. economy went under in 2008. He weathered the storm and SpaceX is a reality.[30] The new kids on the block are the best hope for saving human, plant and animal life on our small planet. Solar panels to lessen green house gases, electric cars not dependent on fossil fuels, sustainable homes and commercial centers as well as co-existence with the environment are understood by world-class entrepreneurs and young people. The environmental challenges of this century will be met by brave entrepreneurs and young people who understand, "it's the environment, stupid". They have the courage of my Spanish and Portuguese ancestors who risked everything to achieve not just financial success but human progress.

As the Space Foundation observes on its website,

"Many nations now recognize the strategic value and practical benefits of space assets and are pursuing space capabilities. By the end of 2010, government, commercial or academic organizations in at least 52 nations — including 19 member states of ESA — were operating one or more satellites, or planning to launch a satellite before the end of 2012. Some of those nations include: Argentina, Australia, Austria, Bolivia, Bulgaria, Chile, Colombia, Czech Republic, Denmark, Egypt, Greece, Indonesia, Kazakhstan, Laos, Luxembourg, Malaysia, Mexico, the Netherlands, Norway, Pakistan, Portugal, Romania, Saudi Arabia, Spain, South Africa, Sweden, Thailand, Turkey, Venezuela and Vietnam."[31]

President Obama's push to commercialize space and open it up to private industry will be the most successful legacy of his presidency. "By the mid-2030s, I believe we can send people to orbit Mars and bring them safely back to Earth. Landing on Mars will follow, and "I expect to be around to see it."[32] The question of who lands on Mars first is for history to decide. As Hernan Cortez observed, "Victories are won by the valiant, not by numbers."

1 "Company." SpaceX. Accessed July 25, 2015. http://www.spacex.com/about.

2 Ibid.

3 Amos, Jonathan. "Mars for the 'average Person' - BBC News." BBC News. March 20, 2012. Accessed July 25, 2015. http://www.bbc.com/news/health-17439490.

4 Ibid.

5 Ibid.

6 Ibid.

7 "Blue Origin." Blue Origin. Accessed July 25, 2015. https://www.blueorigin.com/.

8 Dreyfuss, Bob. "The Costly Failure of Missile Defense." The Nation. July 26, 2013. Accessed July 25, 2015. http://www.thenation.com/article/costly-failure-missile-defense/.

9 Drew, Christopher. "Costliest Jet, Years in Making, Sees the Enemy: Budget Cuts." The New York Times. November 28, 2012. Accessed July 25, 2015. http://www.nytimes.com/2012/11/29/us/in-federal-budget-cutting-f-35-fighter-jet-is-at-risk.html.

10 "Nimitz Class Aircraft Carrier." Wikipedia. Accessed July 25, 2015. http://en.wikipedia.org/wiki/Nimitz-class_aircraft_carrier.

11 Seife, Charles. "The Billionaires' Space Club Is About Ego, Not Exploration." December 30, 2014. Accessed July 25, 2015. http://www.slate.com/articles/health_and_science/space_20/2014/12/billionaires_private_space_rocket_ships_elon_musk_and_richard_branson_go.html.

12 Space X cite supra.

13 "Human Mission to Mars." Wikipedia. Accessed July 25, 2015. http://en.wikipedia.org/w/index.php?title=Human_mission_to_Mars&redirect=no.

14   Smith, O. Glenn, and Paul D. Spudis. "Op-ed | Mars for Only $1.5 Trillion." SpaceNews.com. March 08, 2015. Accessed July 25, 2015. http://spacenews.com/op-ed-mars-for-only-1-5-trillion/.

15   Zubrin, Robert. "Op-ed | Misdirection on Mars." SpaceNews.com. May 04, 2015. Accessed July 25, 2015. http://spacenews.com/op-ed-misdirection-on-mars/.

16   Kaufman, for National Geographic PUBLISHED April 23, 2014, Marc. "A Mars Mission for Budget Travelers." National Geographic. April 23, 2014. Accessed July 25, 2015. http://news.nationalgeographic.com/news/2014/04/140422-mars-mission-manned-cost-science-space/.

17   "Indian Space Research Organization." Wikipedia. Accessed July 25, 2015. http://en.wikipedia.org/wiki/Indian_Space_Research_Organisation.

18   "Brazilian Space Agency." Wikipedia. Accessed July 25, 2015. http://en.wikipedia.org/wiki/Brazilian_Space_Agency.

19   "Guiana Space Centre." Wikipedia. Accessed July 25, 2015. http://en.wikipedia.org/wiki/Guiana_Space_Centre.

20   "JAXA Japan Aerospace Exploration Agency." Wikipedia. Accessed July 25, 2015. http://en.wikipedia.org/wiki/JAXA.

21   Pekkanen, Saadia. "Japan's Evolving Space Program." Japan's Evolving Space Program. September 9, 2011. Accessed July 25, 2015. http://www.nbr.org/research/activity.aspx?id=173.

22   "Iranian Space Agency." Wikipedia. Accessed July 25, 2015. http://en.wikipedia.org/wiki/Iranian_Space_Agency.

23   "Space and Upper Atmosphere Research Commission." Wikipedia. Accessed July 25, 2015. http://en.wikipedia.org/wiki/Space_and_Upper_Atmosphere_Research_Commission.

24   Grammaticas, Damian. "Inside North Korea's Space Centre." BBC News. April 11, 2012. Accessed July 25, 2015. http://www.bbc.com/news/world-asia-china-17684617.

25   "IncludeSwf('/sites/all/themes/asi_tema/flash/logo_en.swf',",'94','94','transparent',",'FHP')." Welcome to A.S.I. Accessed July 25, 2015. http://www.asi.it/en.

26   "How Much Money Is Spent on Space Exploration? (Intermediate) - Curious About Astronomy?" How Much Money Is Spent on Space

Exploration? (Intermediate) - Curious About Astronomy? Ask an Astronomer. Accessed July 25, 2015. http://curious.astro.cornell.edu/about-us/150-people-in-astronomy/space-exploration-and-astronauts/general-questions/921-how-much-money-is-spent-on-space-exploration-intermediateOther sources place the figure at approximately $41 billion. See: "List of Government Space Agencies."Wikipedia. Accessed July 25, 2015. http://en.wikipedia.org/wiki/List_of_government_space_agencies.

27 "WMT Key Statistics | Wal-Mart Stores, Inc. Common St Stock - Yahoo! Finance. Accessed July 25, 2015. http://finance.yahoo.com/q/ks?s=WMT%2BKey%2BStatistics.

28 Wheeler, Winslow T. "America's $1 Trillion National Security Budget." Truthout. March 16, 2014. Accessed July 25, 2015. http://www.truthout.org/news/item/22495-americas-1-trillion-national-security-budget.

29 "List of Government Space Agencies."Wikipedia. Accessed July 25, 2015. http://en.wikipedia.org/wiki/List_of_government_space_agencies. see also: "Global Space Programs" Online at: "Global Space Programs." Global Space Programs. Accessed July 25, 2015. http://www.spacefoundation.org/programs/public-policy-and-government-affairs/introduction-space/global-space-programs.

30 Vance, Ashlee. "Elon Musk's Space Dream Almost Killed Tesla | Bloomberg Business." Bloomberg.com. May 14, 2015. Accessed July 25, 2015. http://www.bloomberg.com/graphics/2015-elon-musk-spacex/?src=longreads.

31 "Global Space Programs." Global Space Programs. Accessed July 25, 2015. http://www.spacefoundation.org/programs/public-policy-and-government-affairs/introduction-space/global-space-programs.

STAFF, NPR. "Mars Or Bust: Putting Humans On The Red Planet." NPR. January 19, 2014. Accessed July 25, 2015. http://www.npr.org/2014/01/19/264030413/mars-or-bust-putting-humans-on-the-red-planet.

CHAPTER 11

It's Always Been Dangerous

La victoria trova cento padri, a nessuno
vuole riconoscere l'insuccesso
— COUNT GIAN GALEAZZO CIANO (1903-1944)

The Columbia shuttle disaster and the deaths of the seven brave astronauts reminded us of the danger of space exploration. The shuttle launches were so common that we mistakenly believed they had become routine. They are not. The short journey to outer space on top of a controlled explosion at 17,500 miles per hour is never to be considered routine. Throughout history, exploration has been and will continue to be fraught with peril.

In previous centuries the dangers came from weather, people defending their homelands from the invading explorers, disease and sometimes mutiny. When Columbus came to this part of the planet, he and his small crew did not have to carry oxygen and life support systems. On Columbus' fourth journey, a disaster occurred. A fleet of 30 ships was allowed to journey back to Spain despite Columbus' warning of a hurricane.

"Columbus made his fourth voyage from Spain to the Americas in 1502. He was such a sure navigator by then that the 3500-mile voyage took a mere 21 days. But he did not arrive happy. At Santo Domingo on June 29 Columbus requested entry into the harbor for his five ships, and he urged the governor to detain a 30-ship fleet ready to sail to Spain. He warned a terrible storm was brewing. The governor and his retinue mocked Columbus as a phony fortune-teller. Not only did the governor order the fleet to sail but denied Columbus entry into the harbor.

"May God take you!' fumed Columbus. That was always his strongest curse. Once again Columbus was thwarted by dull, proud people. He was no gypsy fortune-teller but the sea captain supreme. The mix of oily swells from the southeast, abnormal tide, heaviness in the air, aching arthritis, wispy cirrus clouds streaming high overhead, and a magnificent crimson sunset meant only one thing: a savage hurricane was coming from the north or east! Denied the harbor, Columbus anchored his ships off the southwest shore of the island with protection from north and west. If anchors broke loose the winds would drive them out to sea, not into shore. The 30 ships of the fleet sailed east, then north through the Mona Passage. Barely underway into the Atlantic the gold-laden fleet was hammered by ferocious winds. Within hours 20 ships sank with all hands. Nine others were driven ashore and battered to bits. One ship of the fleet survived. A fortune in gold, 29 ships and 500 men were lost. [1]

Despite this colossal setback, Spanish exploration of the planet continued. The return on investment was not immediate. Sometimes the only thing we get from exploration is more knowledge of what not to do in the future. A careful review of previous explorations reveals that many, if not most of them failed. The successes are well known but like life, when we fail we are often forgotten. After Columbus, a series of explorers and adventurers set forth to the new world. The successful expeditions and conquests of Francisco Pizarro and Hernando de Cortez are required high school history.

The failed expeditions, where lives were lost and no gold or silver was discovered, are not as publicized. Some have landmarks named after them. But humans have short memories. Hudson Bay, named after the failed voyager Henry Hudson, is a classic example.

Henry Hudson was an Englishman and accomplished navigator and sailor. It is unknown where and when he was born, but his four ocean voyages put his name on several places on the global map.

He set sail on his fourth journey from England on April 17, 1610, and headed northwest. The journey was fraught with hardships and threats of mutiny. The weather was foul and the seas icy. The ship, the *Discovery*, made its way through an icy passage known today as the Hudson Strait. (The strait is 450 miles of water separating northern Labrador from Baffin Island.) In August, he sighted a huge body of water that he mistakenly assumed was the Pacific Ocean. This body of water was in fact a large bay later named the Hudson Bay. While exploring, the bay became very icy (in fact it is ice nine months of the year). By November, the ship was frozen in. With dwindling food supplies, Hudson's crew grew increasingly angry, ill, and frozen. Mutiny was on every crew member's mind. When the ship was freed by melting ice, Hudson opted to continue sailing westward. By June 1611, the crew did indeed mutiny. They forced Hudson, his son, and sick and loyal sailors in a small boat. They were never heard from again. Only a handful of sailors made it back to England aboard the *Discovery*. They were not punished for the mutiny.[2]

What Hudson's voyage accomplished was the knowledge that the Northwest Passage to the Orient was not going to be possible because of ice from the Arctic. Many explorers have been forgotten having drowned or become lost, eaten by wild animals or killed by locals protecting their homeland. Among the forgotten was Portuguese explorer João Fernandes Lavrador.

"A small landowner (lavrador) on the island of Terceira in the Azores. The details of his life and voyages are vague and uncertain, but it is known that he had business connections with the port of Bristol, that he was given a royal patent in 1499, and that he made one or more voyages to the New World. It is possible that in 1500 he reached what we know as Greenland, and called it Tiera del Lavrador. The name later migrated south to what is now called Labrador. Fernandes then joined a Bristol syndicate, and it is thought that he was lost on a voyage to America in 1501."[3]

He joins numerous souls who were lost on a voyage to America. Gaspar Corte-Real was given a royal charter in 1500 by the Portuguese to explore Newfoundland. But the venture was a disaster.

"Gaspar sailed to Terra Verde again in 1501, with three caravels. Again, there has been much speculation about his route. He encountered ice, sailed south and found a more temperate land which some locate in Labrador, others — more plausibly — in eastern Newfoundland. The expedition captured about 60 aboriginal people as slaves who were said to "resemble gypsies in colour, features, stature and aspect; are clothed in the skins of various animals …They are very shy and gentle, but well formed in arms and legs and shoulders beyond description …." Only the captives reached Portugal. The others drowned, with Gaspar, on the return voyage.

Gaspar's brother, Miguel Corte-Real, went to look for him in 1502, but also failed to return."[4]

Explorer John Davis sailed south along the Labrador coast in 1586 — two of his men were killed by Inuit John Knight was forced onto the Labrador coast by ice in 1606, where he and three crew members disappeared.[5]

Even if the explorer was successful, he sometimes met his fate at the hands of the perturbed local population. James Cook sailed the world for England in some of the most exciting adventures humans have ever recorded. He and his men had one adventure too many. According to Alistair MacLean:

"Six days later, following a severe storm in which Cook's vessels were severely damaged, the vessels were obliged to return to Hawaii to effect repairs. This time their welcome was less than enthusiastic. There were numerous incidents of petty theft by the natives and when during the night of 13 February one of the ship's cutters was stolen, Cook felt obliged to take some retaliatory action. His custom, when confronted by such circumstances, was to take hostage some senior person in the native hierarchy and hold them until the stolen articles were returned. On the morning of the 14th, Cook went ashore accompanied by some marines to take King Kalaniopu hostage. A party arrived at the King's hut and he agreed to accompany them back to the ship. When they arrived at the beach a large, unruly crowd numbering in the thousands surrounded Cook. Apparently at some point a shot was fired and in the ensuing uproar Cook was clubbed to the ground and repeatedly stabbed by native spears. His body was taken on board his ship and was buried at sea on 22 February, 1779.[6]

After humans conquered the tops of the oceans on flimsy wooden ships and our very few land areas on our tiny planet, humanity's next journey is to space. This journey is far more challenging then fighting each other with sharp sticks and pieces of lead. When Hernan Cortez fought the Aztecs, he and his men and their numerous allies did not have to leave the Earth's orbit with their own oxygen in tiny spaceships to endure a weightless environment. Nothing humans have ever accomplished in previous explorations is as dangerous as space travel.

But persistence will overcome most of life's difficulties and, with careful planning, lead to success. In any endeavor, what separates the losers from the winners is picking yourself back up when you have been knocked down. Spain could simply have given up exploring and colonizing the new world after the loss of that fleet during Columbus' early explorations. Financial success did not come until Cortez and Pizarro brought back very large quantities of gold and silver.

The astronauts and cosmonauts who died trying to take humanity into outer space must be honored with more exploration. More astronauts and cosmonauts are going to die. There will be accidents and loss of life as well as expensive disasters. Three U.S. astronauts died in an Apollo cabin in 1967; four Soviet cosmonauts died in two accidetns in 1967 and 1971; seven astronauts died in the space shuttle Challenger in 1986 and seven more died in the Columbia accident.[7] During launches the men and women who are about to head off to outer space are on top of what amounts to a high explosive with liquid and solid fuel. There will be more accidents and more loss of life. It will continue to be very dangerous. Through out all of human history mankind's story has been one of death and expense in pursuit of exploration. The result has been humans have conquered the planet.

The next step forward is to land men on Mars and colonize that small planet. If America chooses not to go forward with this exploration and colonization, other nations have already decided this is man's destiny. The Russians have asked China to be a partner in a moon base.[8] Europe with Russia's help, China, Japan and now India must be taken seriously as they strive to conquer outer space.

1 "The 4 Voyages of Columbus." The 4 Voyages of Columbus. Accessed July 25, 2015. http://www.carnaval.com/columbus/4voyages.htm.

2 "Myungkun-Thesis1." : Explorers. Accessed July 25, 2015. http://myungkun.blogspot.com/2007/02/christopher-columbus-christopher.html.

3 "The Portuguese Explorers." The Portuguese Explorers. Accessed July 25, 2015. http://www.heritage.nf.ca/articles/exploration/portuguese.php.

4 Ibid.

5 Ibid.

6 Ransor, Eugene L. "The Seaforth Bibliography." Google Books. 2004. Accessed July 26, 2015. https://books.google.com/books?id=8DHAAwAAQBAJ&pg=PA305&lpg=PA305&dq=The%2BDeath%2Bof%2BCaptain%2BCook%2C%2Bby%2BAlistair%2BMacLean&source=bl&ots=kx3BiuOjiY&sig=1MDtUQ6CH7Enq91LdH0SuBScg9U&hl=en&sa=X&ved=0CD4Q6AEwBmoVChMIo8ue3vT3xgIViVmICh2dLAgk#v=onepage&q

=The%20Death%20of%20Captain%20Cook%2C%20by%20Alistair%20
MacLean&f=false.

7 "Encyclopedia Astronautica." Encyclopedia Astronautica. Accessed July
26, 2015. http://www.astronautix.com/.

8 "Russia Invites China to Join in Creating Lunar Station." Moondaily.com.
April 29, 2015. Accessed July 26, 2015. http://www.moondaily.com/
reports/Russia_Invites_China_to_Join_in_Creating_Lunar_Station_999.
html.

CHAPTER 12

Do Plants and Animals Have Souls?

> "Murderers very often start out by
> killing and torturing animals as kids."
> — ROBERT K. RESSLER
> FBI SERIAL KILLER PROFILER

D o plants and animals have souls? This question is important. Had my Spanish ancestors initially believed that Indians were humans, they would not have been able to indiscriminately murder indigenous people. Eventually there was great religious debate in the Catholic Church over whether or not Indians had souls and were human. When after much intellectual Catholic discussion it was decided that Indians were human and had souls, the massive and indiscriminate murders were replaced with political domination in South and Central America. In Seneca Nation, John Mohawk wrote that:

"The Indians presented an interesting dilemma when a dispute between the clergy and the military arose around the identity of the Indians. Bartolome de las Casas, a priest, circulated accounts of Spanish cruelty which were published in Western Europe and eventually became a source of embarrassment to the Spanish crown. The crown then ordered a debate before the Council of the Indies to settle the question whether the American Indians were indeed human beings possessed of a soul, and therefore, rightfully the charges of the Holy Roman Catholic Church, or, as some conquistadors asserted, sub-humans who had no rights whatever. The conquistadors hired Gines de Sepulveda as their attorney. He argued forcefully that Indians are sub-humans. Las Casas argued they had souls and intelligence and can be socialized to be servants of both the crown and the church." [1]

If plants and animals have "souls" then humans cannot indiscriminately slaughter them. Like the indigenous people and later women and blacks, once people had "souls" they also had legal status and could not be treated as property. Plants and animals have to be protected because they exist only on this tiny planet in our solar system. In fact, we need to not only protect plants and animals, we need to go a step further and terra-form Mars and take life to that lifeless planet. In addition to protecting life here, we need to spread human, animal and plant life throughout our solar system. This quest to expand life to our lifeless solar system will create hundreds of millions of jobs, entire new industries and give hope to youths that their future matters.

Our great Earth Mother does not care what we tiny frail little humans believe. Our planet will survive regardless of temperature change. The various species will adapt or die. That is evolution. What matters is a temperature range that allows survival of species we approve of as stewards of the planet. Temperature determines growing cycles and has a dramatic impact on food supplies. With higher water levels from a rising ocean, this will allow for the migration of disease that will kill off millions of people. Unchecked, global warming will have a profound effect on life on our very small planet. Humans will not be the only creatures who will be impacted from this massive climate change. According to "Global Warming, Early Warning Signs":

> "Global temperature in 1998 was the hottest in the historical record, and the temperature increase over the 20th century is likely to be the highest of the past millennium. Global average temperatures have warmed about one degree Fahrenheit (0.6°C) since 1900. The ten warmest years on record have occurred since 1987, seven of them since 1994."[2]

There are no whales, dolphins, mountain gorillas, rhinos, giant pandas, eagles, insects, banana trees or grapes on any of the planets in the inner solar system.

There might be small life forms consisting of bacteria. But complex living beings like mountain lions or cobras exist only on Earth. Humans have been very successful in reproducing. Other animal species have not. Again, our environmental problems result from overpopulation. In a mere two hundred years, humans have increased from one billion to over seven billion. As our population has exploded as a result of better agriculture, urbanization and improved medical practices, the numbers of the various other creatures on our small planet has substantially decreased.

The Earth and all of the ecosystems, complex food chains and natural environments are perfect. There is a natural balance between predators and prey. The only imperfection is humans. Lions kill enough to eat and once full do not slaughter every last animal within their territories. Humans kill every last animal and plant in an ecosystem for short-term pleasure or comfort. If you go to a city, any city anywhere on Earth, there is an abundance of humans, but very little else other than "pets" and favored plants.

Why do humans have so little respect for the plants and animals that exist only on this small planet? One explanation is theological. Under Western Christian thought, humans are at the peak of God's creation and the Earth is viewed as a resource to be exploited and utilized to man's sole advantage. It is this misguided view of Christ and the message of peace that has caused so much harm to nature.

Courtesy Horácio Castro

In <u>The Historical Roots of Our Ecological Crisis</u>, Lynn White, Jr. observes that:

> I personally doubt that disastrous ecologic backlash can be avoided simply by applying to our problems more science and more technology. Our science and technology have grown out of Christian attitudes toward man's relation to nature which are almost universally held not only by Christians and neo-Christians but also by those who fondly regard themselves as post-Christians. Despite Copernicus, all the cosmos rotates around our little globe. Despite Darwin, we are not, in our hearts, part of the natural process. We are superior to nature, contemptuous of it, willing to use it for our slightest whim.

[Ronald Reagan,] the newly elected Governor of California, like myself a churchman but less troubled than I, spoke for the Christian tradition when he said (as is alleged), "when you've seen one redwood tree, you've seen them all." To a Christian a tree can be no more than a physical fact. The whole concept of the sacred grove is alien to Christianity and to the ethos of the West. For nearly 2 millennia Christian missionaries have been chopping down sacred groves, which are idolatrous because they assume spirit in nature. What we do about ecology depends on our ideas of the man-nature relationship. More science and more technology are not going to get us out of the present ecologic crisis until we find a new religion, or rethink our old one.[2]

White's insightful essay and Rachael Carson's <u>Silent Spring</u> started the intellectual framework for rethinking the effects of industrialization and modern technology and man's role in nature. There are limits to growth.

But it is not so much theology that has caused our present difficulties. A modern technological state and a healthy environment are compatible. It is over-population, consumerism and conspicuous consumption that are at the heart of "environmental problems". The pressures on other species came about after the world's population added an extra five billion people in the last two hundred years. These extra five billion people have outgrown the ability of the Earth to provide the natural resources of fish stocks, wild sources of animal proteins like buffalo and elk or zebras. This is why we clear-cut forests, log in tropical jungles, kill wild cats, gorillas, whales and fish cod to near extinction. It is a reason we kill elephants for their tusks. If it comes down to the monkey eats or the human eats, the monkey is either going to starve or the human is going to eat the monkey. Hunger and greed destroy life.

Respect for nature means that when we explore the oceans and outer space we look to the preservation of these other life forms because they have the inherent right to exist simply because they cannot be found anywhere else in the universe. Plants and animals are a special part of God's creation. While Copernicus was right about location of the Earth in relation to the universe, he was mistaken about importance.

Since we clearly know there is no meaningful life outside of the Earth, we need to preserve our diverse life forms and eventually take them with us to the other planets. They will be there to share in our existence. Over several centuries, we can make Mars more habitable and maybe 500 years from now bring life to that empty planet. Transforming a lifeless planet to one that supports Earthly plants, animals, insects, birds, and humans will be an undertaking of epic proportions. Just like exploration of the non-European world was a monumental task 500 years ago.

We know now from study and observation that animals have feelings like fear, sex for pleasure, anger and excitement.[3] Part of the reason for the conclusion that other animals have clear feelings of love, anger and jealousy is that under the veneer of skin coverings the brains and DNA of humans and other primates are very similar. Animals are our evolutionary cousins. We share approximately 98.5 percent of the same DNA as a chimpanzee.[4]

Researchers and pet owners having vast experience around non-humans have observed a variety of emotions among a vast array of animals. In The Smile of a Dolphin, edited by University of Colorado biologist Marc Bekoff, 50 researchers who have spend their careers studying animals including cats, dogs, bears, chimps, whales, elephants and various other creatures have legitimized research on animal emotions.[5]

The researchers have observed chimps die from grief and elephants express joy at reuniting with family groups.[6] Our words cannot properly express what these other creatures are feeling since we do not share the same communication. Animals have their own complex communication. We just don't fully understand how this communications take place or their meanings. Some research is taking place worldwide on what elephants say to each other when they send low frequency waves that humans cannot hear. We know from observation that dolphins work and play together in groups. They make various types and frequencies of sound, many beyond the human ear's ability to hear. We don't yet know what these sounds mean. But with time and research we will learn. Some researchers are making progress. In an excellent CNN story, "There Is More to Animal Communication Than Meets the Ear", correspondent Rusty Dornin talked with various researchers in this area and observed:

> "Kangaroo rats, for example, communicate by stamping their feet. Recordings of their syncopated toe-tapping suggest to researcher Jan Randall that there is more there than just a congenital sense of rhythm.

"What the rat is saying it when it foot-drums an alert is 'I'm alert … I see you … go away.'"

Bio-acoustical engineer Bernie Krause has gone from the equator to the Arctic Circle, eavesdropping on the animal kingdom. He believes animal communication is quite complex.

"I'll see evidence of creatures having exchanges between one another … behavior that kind of relates to vocal communication that's astounding."

Killer whales with accents

(CNN)

Krause says killer whales have detailed chats when on the attack, and that the accent of one pod might be different from that of others.

"There may be groups in the area that have the same language and articulation," Krause said, "but each pod or group of animals has its own vocal accent which is unique to that pod."

Ornithologist Luis Baptista says sparrows sing different dialects in each region. He says birds can also give more than one danger call.

Another researcher says that prairie dogs bark differently depending on the predator. There's one bark for

coyotes, one for hawks and one for humans. The researcher claims there's even one for a human carrying a gun.

Some scientists scoff at such interpretations and
say animals are capable of only the simplest alert calls.
But a growing number agree that talk amongst the animals is anything but dull.[7]

As we learn more from our studies of plants and animals, it becomes clear that these complex evolutionary cousins need protection from humans to survive. If animals have "feelings" and
exist nowhere else in our inner solar system, do we have the
moral right to kill them just because we have the ability? Laws
are evolving to reflect the change in view of man's relationship
with nature. The present Western Christian view is animals are
chattels and people have property rights in these living, breathing
creatures. As Gary L. Francione, law professor at Rutgers states:

"The problem is that human interests are protected by
rights in general and by the right to own property in particular. As far as the law is concerned, an animal is the
personal property, or chattel, of the animal's owner and
cannot possess rights. Indeed, it is a fundamental premise
of our property law that property cannot itself have rights
as against human owners and that, as property, animals are
objects of the exercise of human property rights."[8]

Some of the extreme animal rights groups want this view to
change and consider non-human creatures "companions". We
must be careful not to be anthropomorphic in our studies, but

clearly we have a difficult time measuring human emotions, much less the various feelings of animals.

Those of us who have dogs know they get jealous, angry, happy and like to play. They have a full range of emotions and the intelligence of two-year-old children. They don't care what happens during the day at your office. Dogs are pure happiness. They don't care what is on the news, the latest political scandal or what the stock market is doing. All they are concerned with is they want attention. There are millions of pet owners in the United States and worldwide.

Having pets and plants adds to the mental health of the public. When nursing homes have pets available, the happiness and health of the residents improves. This holistic approach to society makes for a healthier and happier public. Respecting God's creation ultimately results in benefit for humanity. There is theological guidance:

"And God said, Let the waters bring forth abundantly the moving creature that hath life, and fowl that may fly above the earth in the open firmament of heaven. And God created great whales, and every living creature that moves, which the waters brought forth abundantly, after their kind, and every winged fowl after his kind: and God saw that it was good. And God blessed them, saying, Be fruitful, and multiply, and fill the waters in the seas, and let fowl multiply in the earth. And the evening and the morning were the fifth day. And God said, Let the earth bring forth the living creature after his kind, cattle, and creeping thing, and beast of the earth after his kind: and it was so. And God made the beast of the earth after his kind, and cattle after their kind, and every thing that creeps upon the earth after his kind: and God saw that it was good."

GENESIS 2: 20-25[9]

Or this passage from Ecclesiastes 3:19-21:

"Man's fate is like that of the animals; the same fate awaits them both: As one dies, so dies the other. All have the same breath, man has no advantage over the animal. Everything is meaningless. All go to the same place; all come from dust and to dust all return. Who knows if the spirit of man rises upward and if the spirit of the animal goes down into the earth?"[10]

Our armada and Air Force can bomb any nation back to the Stone Age. Our armies can decimate any armed forces brought against us. Now that we have achieved global dominance, we have a moral choice: Use that power with wisdom to protect the plants and animals that exist only on this planet or holocaust.

1 Mohawk, John. "Indian Nations, The United States And Citizenship Part 1." RootsWeb: CHEROKEE-L [Cherokee Circle] Indian Nations, The United States And Citizenship Part 1. 1983. Accessed July 26, 2015. http://archiver.rootsweb.ancestry.com/th/read/CHEROKEE/2008-06/1212820614.

2 Union of Concerned Scientists "About Climate Hot Map." About Climate Hot Map. Accessed July 26, 2015. http://www.climatehotmap.org/about.html.

3 White, Lynn. "The Historical Roots of Our Ecological Crisis." Histori-

cal Roots Ecological Crisis Lynn White Jr. Accessed July 26, 2015. http://www.earthtalktoday.tv/earthtalk-voices/historical-roots-ecological-crisis.html.

4 Pickrell, John. "Humans, Chimps Not as Closely Related as Thought?" National Geographic. September 24, 2002. Accessed July 26, 2015. http://news.nationalgeographic.com/news/2002/09/0924_020924_dnachimp.html.

5 Bekoff, Marc. "The Smile of a Dolphin." Google Books. October 10, 2000. Accessed July 26, 2015. https://books.google.ca/books/about/The_smile_of_a_dolphin.html?id=U50XAQAAIAAJ.

6 Ibid. There are several very good stories about animals that have literally died of grief. Jane Goodall talks about a chimp that is so depressed on the death of his mother that he waits by her body until he dies.

7 Dornin, Rusty. "There Is More to Animal Communication than Meets the Ear." CNN. September 11, 1997. Accessed July 26, 2015. http://www.cnn.com/TECH/9709/11/animal.communication/.

8 Francione, Gary L., and Robert Garner. "The Animal Rights Debate: Abolition or Regulation?" Abolitionist Approach. 2010. http://www.abolitionistapproach.com/books/the-animal-rights-debate-abolition-or-regulation/#.VbRw8kvBduY.

9 Genesis 2:20-25." Genesis 2:20-25 NIV. Accessed July 26, 2015. https://www.biblegateway.com/passage/?search=Genesis%2B2%3A20-25&version=NIV.

10 "BibleGateway." Ecclesiastes 3:19-21 N. Accessed July 26, 2015. https://www.biblegateway.com/passage/?search=Ecclesiastes%2B3%3A19-21&version=N.

CHAPTER 13

Young People Can Save the World

> "I follow my passion. I think it is very
> important to follow your passion.
> Don't listen to what everyone else
> says, follow your passion."
> — JAMES CAMERON
> FILMMAKER, EXPLORER, ADVENTURER

The world needs to listen and follow the advice of scientists like Dr. Daniel Pauly, conservationist Jane Goodall, filmmaker/explorer James Cameron and numerous others. There is not much time left. The sharks of the ocean are the top predator. They are being slaughtered to make shark fin soup.[1] This practice can be stopped. When the human population was under 1 billion and technology was limited with wooden boats fishing close to shore, killing sharks for their fins, while repulsive, was not going to destroy the food chain and alter the ecosystem. Today, sharks have no chance.

Credit: Fiona Ayerst/Marine Photobank

Japan continues to kill whales under the completely false premise that they are doing "research". Norway, Russia and Iceland are also whale killers.

File:Japan Factory Ship Nisshin Maru Whaling Mother and Calf.jpg Uploaded by Grolltech Created: February 6, 2008[3]

"A whale and a calf being loaded aboard a factory ship, the *Nisshin Maru*. The sign above the slipway reads, "Legal research under the ICRW". Australia released this photo to challenge that claim. In November 2014, Japan announced that it would resume hunting whales in the Southern Ocean, but that it would reduce its catch target by two-thirds. Japan's Fisheries Agency said that Japan intends to catch 333 minke whales each year between 2015 and 2027, down from 935 minke and 50 fin whales. It said the hunts were needed for collecting scientific data and were exempt from a 1986 international ban on commercial whaling, despite the ICJ ruling".[2]

When the politicians of Japan, the world's third-largest economic power, have no regard for sea life, the rest of the world suffers the consequences. The Japanese government has made it clear that it will not respect international scientific consensus that continued whaling is not for scientific research. As Virginia Morell reports in Science Insider:

> "In an unprecedented move, an expert panel that advises the International Whaling Commission's (IWC's) Scientific Committee has rejected Japan's latest plan for resuming the killing of minke whales in the Antarctic. Japan, however, says it will continue with its whaling plans."[4]

The Japanese are a modern society with important traditions. One is respect and use of good manners. One solution to ending Japanese whaling and killing of dolphins is to politely ask this government to end the slaughter. Make the case to the Japanese government that dolphins and whales are highly intelligent creatures with complex social systems, their own communication and killing them because we can is a crime against nature and future generations.

If that does not work, put economic pressure on this government and their industries. A global consumer boycott of whaling and dolphin-killing nations will stop the slaughter faster than you can say sushi. Despite the claims of "tradition," there are Japanese activists working to ban whaling and killing of dolphins. As Shaun O'Dwyer reported: "Junichi Sato and Toru Suzuki, two Greenpeace Japan activists, were convicted of trespass and theft in 2010 after seizing a parcel of whale meat illicitly posted by a Japan scientific whaling employee, which they presented as evidence to prove allegations of embezzlement within the scientific whaling program."[5] These Japanese environmentalists put their freedom on the line to stop the slaughter.

Japanese leaders are like politicians everywhere. They bow to powerful interest groups, more interested in money than the environment; meanwhile the slaughter continues. What will work in stopping the slaughter of the oceans is a global consumer boycott of Japanese goods and public protests before Japanese embassies. This can be done through social media and public awareness should be pursued immediately by environmental groups working together. Japan, Norway, Russia and Iceland will stop killing whales when their greedy leaders suffer the consequences of the vicious policies that are causing so much harm to the oceans.

Despite political support of whale and dolphin hunting by Japan, Norway, Russia and Iceland, young people and environmentalists in these countries are opposed to the slaughter. Some environmentalists from whaling countries have won prestigious international awards for their environmental work. The Russian environmentalist Dmitry Lisitsyn won the Goldman Environmental Prize in 2011.[6] The Goldman award is the equivalent of the Nobel Prize, for environmental work.

He works hard to stop whaling on Sakhalin Island, a critical breeding area for endangered Western Pacific Gray whales and the Pacific Ocean's most productive salmon spawning ground.

It is the planet's youths who understand their future is at stake. They are making progress in environmental/conservation issues all over the world. Young people use social media and spread the message in a hurry. Facebook has over 1 billion users. China, Russia, India, Brazil, all have social media. This new communication spreads the word about environmental or other issues.

If these governments refuse to stop killing dolphins and whales, the issue can be forced with a consumer boycott. Consumers in a capitalist economy have the power to change the world. A consumer boycott on Earth Day in April will cause any government to immediately take notice. The value of killing dolphins and whales is far less than the economic damage of a one-day boycott of all products from whale and dolphin hunting nations. Add protests at their embassies all over the world and this economic and political pressure will yield some results.

The same consumer boycott power can be used to stop the slaughter of the sharks for Asian shark fin soup. The tradition in Asian societies of serving shark fin soup at important functions like weddings and as a symbol of wealth and success is killing the oceans to produce this delicacy for families that don't understand or don't care about the devastation they are doing.

The sharks are caught and while still alive their fins are cut off. Then they are thrown back into the oceans unable to swim or defend themselves. It is cruel and disgusting behavior. There are cultures out there that have absolutely no regard for any living species. Killing sharks, dolphins, whales, tuna and hunting them to extinction is not viewed as wrong.

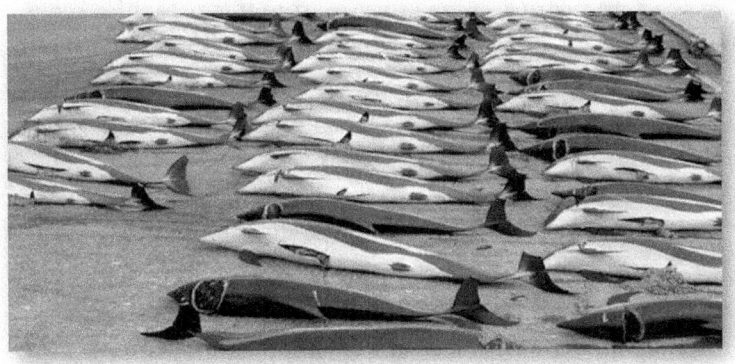

Whales And Dolphins Wikipedia #6

There is no common view of the natural world among the planet's many ethnic groups. Some cultures eat dogs, while others have them as pets. Japan protested that the ban on whaling was cultural racism since the complaints against them were the strongest. Norway, Russia and Iceland hunt whales but Japan was singled out.[7]

When traditional societies were whaling in tiny wooden boats with spears it was almost a fair fight. Whalers were often killed and there were thousands of the magnificent whales. As technology progressed and humans were no longer whaling in tiny wooden boats but now in huge steel ships with cannons and harpoons loaded with explosives, the whales, like all other flesh creatures, did not have a chance.

This nonsense by the small Japanese whaling community that their "tradition" should be preserved would make some sense if they were fishing in Japanese waters in small wooden boats like their ancestors. That is not what is happening. Japanese whalers are in large modern ships and the whales have absolutely no chance whatsoever to survive from their "tradition". They kill whales all over the world. Just as the Saudi royal family mistreats women in the name of "tradition" and the Taliban shot a young girl in the face to prevent her from getting an education, there are some traditions that must end. Whaling, killing dolphins and emptying the oceans of sea life is inexcusable.

Whales are a living treasure as are all of the Creators' beautiful creatures that exist only on our tiny planet. Killing dolphins, tuna, swordfish, marlin, sailfish and cleansing the oceans of life is immoral and a crime against future generations. It has to be stopped and the governments who are subsidizing these commercial fishing and whaling and killing of dolphins are making a huge mistake for short-term votes and industry profits. Education and public awareness can stop the slaughter of the oceans.

The global community does not share Japan's view that slaughtering whales with high-tech ocean-going vessels using harpoons with explosives is "traditional". We see it as the complete nonsense it is. Slaughtering whales and dolphins and emptying out the oceans has nothing to do with "tradition" — it is a choice. Killing baby seals was viewed as a tradition. That does not mean it is acceptable.

Young people in Asia and all over the world are working to end whaling, dolphin killing, destruction of the oceans, and shark finning. Sports figures and prominent businessmen are advocating the end of shark fin soup. Some governments are responding to the public awareness campaigns. WildAid, an environmental conservationist non-profit organization based out of San Francisco has been at the forefront of working to educate people about the harm to the oceans caused by shark fin soup. Working with other conservation groups, their public awareness campaign is having positive results. In their words:

> "An estimated 100 million sharks are killed every year with fins from up to 73 million used for shark fin soup, primarily to supply the market in Mainland China. A pair of shark fins can sell for as much as US$700 per kg in Asia. Some shark populations have declined by up to 98% in the last 15 years and nearly one-third of pelagic sharks species are considered threatened by the International Union for the Conservation of Nature.

> Our latest campaign features several new PSAs including sports icon David Beckham, actor and director Jiang Wen, and actress Maggie Q."

> "Our campaigns, in combination with government bans at official events, have contributed to a reported 50%-70% decrease in China's shark fin consumption."[8]

The Chinese government has banned shark fin soup from state functions.[9]

Environmental groups like Fins Attached, Shark Savers, Shark Angels, Shark Whisperer and the Sea Shepherd Conservation Society, as well as WildAid, the World Wildlife Fund, GreenPeace, the Nature Conservancy, BiteBack and numerous foundations and research institutes are spreading the message.

In 2011, President Obama signed the Shark Conservation Act that closes loopholes to obtain shark fins.[9] This change in the law ended shark fin soup in the United States. The same thing needs to be done globally. The Law of the Sea Convention needs to be amended to ban shark finning, whaling and killing dolphins as well as creating a Global High Seas Marine Preserve.

What makes this environmental campaign difficult is the life being protected are underwater. People can't see under the oceans and understand the devastation caused by shrimp trawlers scraping the bottom of all life. The commercial vessels far out to sea cannot be seen slaughtering tens of thousands of creatures and discarding them as "by-catch". There is no park ranger out in the oceans issuing citations and making arrests. Here is where changes can be made. Navies of various nations can enforce the ban and protect the fish stocks.

Changing cultural habits that have taken several centuries to develop can be accomplished with careful use of media resources. Shark fin soup is more a tradition than a food. So is racism and homophobia a "tradition," but that does not mean it can't be ended. Slavery has been pretty much eradicated. Women vote and hold high office in civilized parts of the planet. Environmental laws have been passed. Change is not only possible but continuous.

The aircraft carrier battle groups we discussed earlier are expensive. The U.S.S. Gerald Ford, a Nimitz class aircraft carrier, cost over $12 billion dollars to build. The carriers project military power. To what end? As numerous scholars have noted, intervention in poor countries by rich countries is a failure. Having great military power and the ability to project it across the world does not mean foreign intervention will be successful. Vietnam, Algeria, Angola, Cuba, Cambodia, Iraq all show foreign intervention by rich nations failed.[10]

Projecting military power will not save the fish stocks. Where these carriers are based is a political and economic decision that cannot be ignored. Without the 6th fleet, San Diego, even with its tremendous weather, would have a tough time economically. Camp Pendleton is north of San Diego. Like the rest of America, Southern California spends lots of money on defense and little on space and ocean exploration. This is why there has to be an economically and politically viable alternative to defense spending. Young people graduating from college and high school cannot be left without quality high-tech jobs.

The transition from defense spending to exploration can be accomplished by placing NOAA and NASA under the jurisdiction of the Department of Defense. NASA needs to be administered and funded by the U. S. Air Force. NOAA needs to be administered and funded by the U.S. Navy. These branches of the armed forces have larger budgets, contracting experience and the administrative personnel to manage these important agencies. Then these agencies will get the proper funding to pursue their missions and communities like San Diego will not lose jobs. In fact, new jobs will be created. New industries will rise up from exploring the oceans and the solar system.

Since the exploration of the oceans, Mars and the asteroid belt will be extremely dangerous it is important that like in ancient times this should be a military adventure. Cortez and Pizarro were soldiers as were almost all early Spanish explorers. With the vast array of global bases, this transition is ideally suited to work with many nations to explore the inner solar system. Communities like Hill Air Force Base in Ogden, Utah, can repair service modules to Mars rather than their current functions that include maintaining our ICBMs. This redirection of the military mission from the Cold War and the War on Terror to exploration of the oceans and inner solar system will avoid the shock of unemployment to the U.S. economy that is so heavily dependent on the arms race and war as economic policy. Again, we cannot just "cut" defense spending.

The transition from aircraft carrier battle groups to small patrol boats based out of San Diego will prevent unemployment and create new industries. Shipyards will get new work in building the right product for the exploration of the oceans. The U.S. Navy can stop shark finning and over-fishing with the right ships. High seas patrol boats can engage in high-speed chases with sea poachers and board trawlers for inspection.

The United States can change its entire defense budget and cost structure by gifting aircraft carrier battle groups to other nations. Give one aircraft carrier battle group to the Japanese, one to Australia, one to South Korea, two to the European Union, one to Brazil and keep four carrier battle groups.

Unfortunately, China and Russia continue to be aggressive and military power is a reality of life. Defense of the Free World should be a shared cost with our allies, not the United States shouldering the majority of the burden of stopping Chinese and Russian aggression toward other nations. The Chinese aggression in Tibet is real, as is the Russian invasion of the Ukraine, even if it was brought about by Western interference in that country. Young people have to live with last century's leaders who still have a vision of empire and military glory. That can change.

We live in a missile age. Losing one of these carriers would be a national tragedy. The better solution is share the cost of global defense with our allies. Save costs in this age of deficits by gifting these expensive weapon systems. They are operational, expensive to operate and maintain and are outdated antiques from the last century.

Transitioning to high seas patrol boats and research vessels for NOAA and the Coast Guard is practical. Sea power is a choice. In an interconnected world where problems require cooperation not conflict, like it or not we have to build ships that can enforce a global ban on high seas commercial fishing. The companies that build these floating airports are also capable of building more research vessels for NOAA, deep-sea exploration and mining vessels and high-speed boats to patrol and catch poachers.

They can also build effective spaceships for the exploration and colonization of Mars and beyond. This shift in policy from defense to exploration will create jobs for the university students in engineering, oceanography, biology, physics and numerous other disciplines. Young people deserve to have hope about their future.

A Trident submarine can launch 192 nuclear warheads on any nation. The United States has 14 of these Ohio class submarines.[11] None of these impressive machines can save the tuna stocks or stop whales and dolphins from being slaughtered. Again, none of these nuclear submarines can do ocean mining or research. America can bomb any country on Earth. But that does not help the environment or the economy or provide a future for young people. A Trident submarine and $5.00 will buy you a cup of coffee.

Even one thermonuclear warhead destroying one city any-where on Earth would be a tragedy of unimaginable propor-tions. One U.S. or Russian submarine can effectively destroy civilization. We can also destroy civilization by collapsing the ecosystem. Even without nuclear war, losing the environment war with nature will still result in the extinction of all species on this unique and tiny planet.

Young people today were not around when these Cold War weapons were invented. These nuclear submarines were built at a time when the Soviet Union was on the other side of the Cold War. Today China is the United States' second-largest trading partner. Bombing China is not practical and is ridiculous. The Chinese are among the largest holders of U.S. bonds. Any at-tack on China is in reality an attack on the United States. The two economies are so completely intertwined they are in real-ity one global economy with two governments and millions of moving parts and tens of thousands of companies engaged in trade.

The youth of the world need to jointly clean the oceans of plastic. All nations that have navies need to build patrol boats that can enforce a global ban on commercial fishing on the high seas. China, the United States, Russia, Taiwan, the European Union may be trade rivals but all of these nations need to close the high seas to commercial fishing and clean the oceans.

These countries have the ship-building capacity neces-sary to create patrol vessels. The universities exist to produce the highly skilled workers for the new industries of deep sea mining, wild life preservation, oceanography, underwater ar-cheology and numerous other new jobs. What is not there is the political will to transform the World War II and Cold War weapons to patrol boats, research vessels and mining vessels. How can young people make this transition? Public awareness begins at home. Educate family and friends and get involved to make change happen. Young people deserve an opportunity at a future where sea life still exists.

The only way the grip on the taxpayer dollar can be shifted from outdated weapons systems to protecting the oceans is for young people to vote to use the same communities and same defense contractors. General Dynamics Electric Boat division builds the Ohio class nuclear submarines.[12] There is no demand for these vessels other than that created by Congress for employment in their districts. Consequently, only the ongoing basing and maintenance of these ships provides economic activity. That does not create more jobs for young people in this century. What these weapons in fact do is endanger humanity.

Having General Dynamics' electric boat division build deep-sea mining and research vessels will create new jobs for young people graduating from the many fine universities in Rhode Island and Connecticut. Small companies will benefit as suppliers and a multiplier effect will ripple throughout the economy.

Unlike space exploration, where the return on investment will take decades or longer, the return on investment from ocean exploration will be almost immediate. Saving the fish stocks alone is worth billions. The return on investment will come from the immense mineral wealth that lies under the waves as well as saving the fish stocks. Mining of the oceans is already starting to happen. America can miss this new huge market by continuing on its present course. Or policy can shift and young workers can obtain the benefits of deep-sea mining and exploration. These minerals also include diamonds off the coasts of South Africa and Namibia as well as deposits of tin, titanium and gold along the shores of Africa, Asia and South America.[13]

Newport News shipbuilding facility is owned by giant defense contractor Northrop Grumman and located in Newport News, Virginia. Clearly this great company can build another Nimitz aircraft carrier. But they can also build research vessels for NOAA's expanded role in saving the oceans. American shipyards and defense contractors can build *anything!* They need to build new industries for young people for this century.

We baby boomer generation managed to not blow up the world. But we left an absolute mess of an environment and a crowded planet. This mess can only be cleaned up by the young people working with their friends all over the world. It will take decades to undo the massive damage that has been done to the environment. This task is an opportunity to re-industrialize America and bring back millions of high-paying, meaningful jobs for the hundreds of thousands of young people graduating every year from colleges, universities and high schools.

The massive amount of garbage in the oceans is a problem that has received some minor attention. The cleanup can be accomplished in a fairly short time frame. The United States can lead the world in a global campaign involving university and high school students to clean the oceans. This labor-intensive campaign should include the world's militaries. It does not take much skill to go to the beaches of every part of the world and pick up the plastic garbage. High school and college students globally can as part of their curriculum and a requirement for graduation clean the environment. Jail and prison labor can also be used to go to beaches and just clean them. Picking up garbage is labor intensive work which will create low-skill jobs for the millions and millions of people all over the world who are currently unemployed. It will also create high-skill jobs on re-using the recovered materials to create new products from the recycling transforming the global economies to sustainability.

If you don't want the oceans to be full of garbage, quit dumping trash into the seas! It's really that simple. This goal of keeping the oceans and beaches clean can be accomplished with a massive public relations campaign. Having a clean community is a choice made by the people who live there. Some communities demand clean streets, yards, parks and beaches; others don't. We see this pattern all over the world.

Mazatlan, Mexico, used to be a trashy resort city where the beaches were disgusting and full of garage. Today, under the leadership of Mayor Alejandro Higuera Osuna, the beaches and city are clean and safe. His wife Sylvia helps the World Access Project deliver wheelchairs and hold a sports camp for people with disabilities. Again, it is a community choice to be clean, modern and safe. Jobs are created for the people who live in Mazatlan and from the increase in tourism from the nice hotels and clean beaches. The fishing is wonderful and the sea life is carefully managed.

It is great fun to watch the dolphins swim to shore alongside the surfers in Mazatlan. Since Mexico protects its fisheries, the dolphins feel safe enough to interact with the tourists and locals and play with them. You can also see them from shore when you are at your hotel enjoying a break from cold weather. It's not unusual to see people on shore put beached sea rays back in the water.

Other communities are not as clean. When you travel to South Beach, Florida, during spring break, you witness truly disgusting, "trashy pigs gone wild". The beaches are full of trash from the students on spring break. They party and just throw their litter everywhere. If college students on spring break trashed California's pristine beaches, the locals would beat them up and have them arrested. The people from California pride themselves on having clean, wonderful beaches. Miami, Ft. Lauderdale and other eastern Florida communities are dirty.

It is not uncommon to see garbage all over beaches on the west coast of Florida. Contrast those communities with Sarasota and Dustin, Florida. Their beaches are clean and beautiful. This same pattern exists all over the world. Some communities choose to be very clean and safe, like Seaside, Oregon- others are disgusting, like the ungovernable Somalia. The same is true of people's homes and lives. Being trashy is a choice. To have a healthy planet, have healthy people in healthy communities. Sao Tome and Rwanda are poor. But they are very clean countries that can give lessons to developing nations on cleanliness. Their traffic and street lights work and their Internet is high quality. Their hotels are as nice as any in the developed world.

Young people can effectuate all of these changes by doing something very simple in democratic societies- VOTE. The failed extremist politicians who believe the world is going to end and consequently don't care about the future all have term limits. These term limits are called elections. In a democracy, politicians are your elected employees. They are supposed to work for you. If you do not like the job they are doing, fire them. It is that simple. Money does not control politics, votes do.

Obviously you can see the job your politicians are doing with the results of their work or lack of it. The fish stocks are collapsing. The "war on drugs" and the "war on terror" are ruining the planet. The politicians are not stopping the slaughter of the oceans. These politicians can all be fired by voting them out of office in the democracies of the world. In the countries where voting is not possible like China- economic pressure of consumer boycotts can and will change their behavior. Despite the lack of democratic traditions, China is different.

The Chinese government has some very intelligent people in charge. Their work in saving Pandas from extinction, banning shark fin soup from state dinners and now working on global climate change is prudent leadership. Despite the mythology in the West, Chinese leaders do care about the environment, listen to the wants of their massive population and are willing to work to solve international problems. They are trying to solve extremely difficult environmental issues yet continue with economic growth that has done wonders in pulling millions of people out of poverty and made China the second largest economy on the planet. [14]

Young people often feel powerless and do not realize how much power they really have. Youth can make a difference in the global society by making a difference in their world. If you don't buy plastic water bottles irresponsible companies like Coca Cola will quit making them. Americans use on average 167 plastic bottles each year but only recycle 38. [15]

If you don't recycle then, yes, this plastic trash will pollute the Earth. Almost 90 percent of municipal solid waste is packaging and virtually all of it can be recycled. Vote in politicians who will change the laws and make recycling mandatory worldwide. There is no reason other than laziness for homes or communities to be trashy. Criminals that belong to international crime organizations Al Qaeda, the Taliban, Boko Haram, ISIS, drug dealers and others have one thing in common besides false religious beliefs. They are trashy, dirty, hairy, illiterate and want a world that is a garbage dump. Being clean is not a priority to people engaged in crime and violence.

Again these are individual choices. How we choose to live our lives is what will ultimately save the living planet. Young people, please be confident. The future is only hopeless if you quit and do nothing. You can do it. It will just require getting involved and working together with friends from all over the world.

---

1 Ayerst, Fiona. "Finned Sharks in South Africa." Ocean Portal. http%3A%2F%2Focean.si.edu%2Focean-photos%2Ffinned-sharks-south-africa.

2 "Whaling in Japan."Wikipedia. Accessed July 26, 2015. http://en.wikipedia.org/wiki/Whaling_in_Japan. See also "The History of Whaling." Into The Blue. May 04, 2015. Accessed July 26, 2015. http://marinebiology.co/2015/05/04/a-brief-history-of-whaling/.

3 File:Japan Factory Ship Nisshin Maru Whaling Mother and Calf.jpg Uploaded by Grolltech Created: February 6, 2008

4 Morell, Virginia. "Japan Says It Will Hunt Whales Despite Science Panel's Opposition." ScienceInsider. April 16, 2015. http%3A%2F%2Fnews.sciencemag.org%2Fasiapacific%2F2015%2F04%2Fjapan-says-it-will-hunt-whales-despite-science-panel-s-opposition.

5 O'DWYER, SHAUN. "Japanese Activists Fight against the Tide to save Whales and Dolphins | The Japan Times." Japan Times RSS. March 16, 2015. Accessed July 26, 2015. http://www.japantimes.co.jp/community/2015/03/16/voices/japanese-activists-fight-tide-save-whales-dolphins/#.VWgBskvBduY.

6 "Pacific Environment : Russian Environmental Hero Dmitry Lisitsyn Wins Goldman Award." Pacific Environment : Russian Environmental Hero Dmitry Lisitsyn Wins Goldman Award. April 11, 2011. Accessed July 26, 2015. http://pacificenvironment.org/russian-environmental-hero-wins-goldman-award.

7 "International Court Harpoons Japanese Whaling." HubPages. May 4, 2014. Accessed July 26, 2015. http://pacampobasso.hubpages.com/hub/Japanese-Whaling-in-the-Pacific.

8 "Sharks." WildAid. Accessed July 26, 2015. http://www.wildaid.org/sharks.

9 "Shark Conservation Act" The Shark Conservation Act (P.L. 111-348) was introduced in January 2009 by Representative Madeleine Bordallo (D-GU) in the House of Representatives and Senator John Kerry (D-MA) in the Senate in April 2009. The long-awaited bill was approved by both chambers by unanimous consent on the last days of the 111th Congress in December 2010. President Obama signed the bill into law on January 5, 2011. "Shark Conservation Act." Shark Conservation Act. Accessed July 26, 2015. https://awionline.org/content/shark-conservation-act.

10 Schell, Jonathan. "The Iraq Invasion, Ten Years Later." The Nation. March 13, 2013. Accessed July 26, 2015. http://www.thenation.com/article/173338/iraq-invasion-ten-years-later?page=0%2C1#.

11 "OHIO CLASS SUBMARINE." Wikipedia. Accessed July 26, 2015. http://en.wikipedia.org/wiki/Ohio-class_submarine.

12 Ibid.

13 "World Ocean Review." World Ocean Review. Accessed July 26, 2015. http://worldoceanreview.com/en/wor-1/energy/marine-minerals/.

14 Lallanilla, Marc. "China's Top 6 Environmental Concerns." LiveScience. March 15, 2013. Accessed July 26, 2015. http://www.livescience.com/27862-china-environmental-problems.html.

15 "Bottled Water Facts." Ban the Bottle RSS. Accessed July 26, 2015. https://www.banthebottle.net/bottled-water-facts/.

CHAPTER 14

A Future That Works

> "History is not 'just one damn fact
> after another,' as a cynic put it. There
> really are broad patterns to history."
> —— JARED DIAMOND

There are solutions. To a carpenter, all problems can be solved with hammers and nails. To a policeman, the solutions are more arrests and jails. As an attorney, I believe law is the solution to many of the difficulties facing our tiny planet. The "rule of law" has many benefits — the primary one being civilization. A future that works is one based upon international law to govern human behavior. Fortunately, that is the direction we are going. We live in an age where international law is finally starting to take off. It's taken a while, but international law is working and makes life better.

International contracts are honored. Consequently, global trade flourishes. We drink Argentine wine at Thai restaurants. Our clothes come from Honduras and our cars with parts from all over the world are manufactured in Japan. We drink Mexican beer while watching players from all over the world at the U.S. Open. We use our Korean-made phones to call friends in Canada, Central America, Europe and Asia.

Our computers access newspapers from India, Egypt, Israel and South Africa and we have friends from Brazil and Mexico as well as numerous other countries. Again, we are 22 hours from any major city on Earth. Many of us have been to several countries. We have rugs from Afghanistan as well as art pieces from Costa Rica and Rwanda.

Our planet is tiny. Several of us have traveled around the world more than once. Almost all of us have friends or relatives from other countries. When we watch the World Cup, we see athletes participate from all over the world. The same is true of the Pan American Games and numerous international mass spectator events. These are made possible because of communications satellites that have resulted from human space exploration. Even new sports like wheelchair tennis, has international participation that was never possible before in human history. This is the result of jet travel, modern medicine and also by-products of the space program.

There are so many international business deals they can no longer be counted. Trade flourishes all over the world between poor countries, across oceans and borders. From international mining deals in Bolivia to tourists riding elephants in Thailand, international law has made more travel and trade possible than at any time in history. The developing world becomes richer and their economies more modern. As we become more interconnected we use international law every day. The result is life is better. Yes, there are environmental problems and international criminals, but this is the best time in human history to be alive. Much of our current technology is from prior spending on space exploration. The spending has resulted in small computers, better jet travel, major medical breakthroughs and global communication, as well as a map application for our cell phones.

There are standards for numerous products, services and even electricity that are set by the International Standards Organization. In its words, "International Standards make things work. They give world-class specifications for products, services and systems, to ensure quality, safety and efficiency. They are instrumental in facilitating international trade." Over 160 countries are members of this non-governmental organization[1].

This is just one of hundreds of international organizations that makes life better in this century. The result is the terrific world we live in with huge opportunity, as well as big problems and international criminals claiming to be "religious" who would destroy it all.

Companies from all over the world trade on the New York Stock Exchange. Money is invested all over the world at the speed of light and governments cannot keep up with this important change. With the push of a button, money leaves one country and works in another one. The nation state is often powerless to control the speed of capital. Tax havens all over the world pop up like mushrooms after a rain as they try to capture fleeing capital. Never has money been able to move this fast and create so many opportunities yet cause so many problems. From running illegal drugs to small arms traffic to the legal markets of international trade, money is moving. International law can't keep up.

A future that works involves ending this "War on Terror." It ends when the global community stops calling it "terror" and starts calling it "crime". This requires working toward a common international legal system. The World Court is the ideal forum to try individuals who are committing these crimes. Obviously, this will involve hundreds of thousands of trials. There is successful precedence for the use of law as an approach.

The United States has another failed war, "the war on drugs". Over 2.4 million people are in jail and/or prison, all of whom have been processed legally. These people had access to the courts. Fortunately, there are not yet 2.4 million people bombing churches, mosques, restaurants and shooting young girls to prevent them from learning. There are thousands of international criminals, not millions. But if the "War on Terror" continues, there will be millions. Each drone strike and bomb that kills innocent people creates new recruits seeking revenge over the death of their loved ones.

This criminal cancer will metastasize and bring down numerous governments. People who believe they have nothing to lose are not afraid to lose everything, including their lives. Education, employment and intelligent detective work, not drone strikes will turn the tide and change the course of history. Arrest the accused and no one else. Don't kill bystanders just because you can. This creates hate and violence. People who would otherwise remain bystanders then join religious criminal extremists.

Here the mass media can help. Publicity is the jet fuel for criminals. As these criminals see themselves on CNN, FOX News and others, they gain notoriety and followers. But for the media that gives losers a "cause," they would remain pathetic and unknown. When someone is correctly called out as a "criminal," they are not viewed as favorably by social media and the impressionable, discontented youth of the world. The mass media has an obligation to show the crimes and the trials as well as the punishments. That, too, can sell commercial time. Words are powerful. A "criminal" has a far different meaning than a "terrorist". A "terrorist" is a political label.

The politics behind people's crimes is irrelevant. Kidnapping young women, bombing restaurants, killing policemen, these are all crimes committed by thugs who have no interest in the rule of law or something so simple as clean clothes and a shower. Make them appear in court in proper and clean attire. Force them to bathe and neatly trim their beards when they appear before the judiciary. Demand that they treat the institution of law with respect.

These criminals are not interested in the World Cup, tennis, art, science, music, museums, history or any of the benefits that come with having a modern civilized society. They want power only for power's sake and will use religion or any ideology to achieve their demented goal. The members of Al Qaeda, ISIS, Boko Haram and other criminal organizations do not file patents, create public companies, manufacture products, copyright songs and movie scripts or invent new medicines to make the world a better place. Their only skill is crime like murder, kidnapping, bombing restaurants, shooting young girls trying to get an education. They cannot compete in sporting events so they kill athletes. Being the cowards they are, they mask their faces and hide in the shadows. Cowards don't need to be feared, they need to be arrested.

Whatever behavior you feed grows. The mistake the mass media and politicians make is they feed this behavior by giving criminals major television airtime and front-page coverage of important newspapers. While it is understandable that the media like any other business must make money, it is irresponsible to inflate the criminal acts and make them political. There is plenty of room in prison for the world's criminals. Public trials where the accused are properly defended and tried before impartial judges and evidence is presented will work over the long run.

The clear advantage of trials is when people are found innocent and are properly treated with dignity and respect, they will go back to their villages and explain that in fact they did not commit any crimes and the legal system worked in their case. If they engage in criminal acts again, eventually they will be caught, tried and punished appropriately.

In order to implement law across international boundaries, rich nations are going to have to help poor countries develop their legal systems. This is happening. The U.S. Department of Justice and the State Department work actively with other countries in developing legal systems. These programs need to be expanded and receive more media attention. The "rule of law" is an important tool for peace.

Murder, kidnapping, bombing restaurants and shooting school girls are crimes in every civilized country on Earth. The real problem is the justice systems in many parts of the planet are just too impoverished to prosecute criminals. Police officers can be bought off and the public has no confidence in the legal system. Law is a belief system based upon the shared perception of reality of the members of that particular society. When people don't believe in "rules," there are none.

The lack of law is one of the root causes of poverty and suffering on our tiny planet. Countries like Somalia have no functioning government and no legal system. Consequently, they have massive poverty. "No one owns anything," says Abda Azziz, a port worker. "Your land is your land until someone takes it from you, your car your car until it is stolen — that is the law in this country."[2] The United States produces too many attorneys. While there is no legal work here, the world needs more attorneys.

With law, the developed world can help the developing world build clean water systems and functioning toilets. Millions of people have no access to fresh water, much less flush toilets. Approximately 750 million people don't have clean water and over 1 billion do not use toilets.[3]

Stopping "terrorism" is a matter of changing the game to our rules where people learn that regardless of where you are on the planet, if you kill, kidnap, shoot people, torture others or bomb restaurants, you will be prosecuted and, if found guilty, punished. This will require the rich countries to make a concerted effort to economically develop and fully integrate the developing world into the international legal system.

A future that works will also require rich nations to obey international law. It can no longer be "do was we say, not as we do." When the United States attacks other countries in clear violation of international law, as was the case in the Iraq war, all rules fall apart. Global solutions in this century are not technological but political. This involves diplomacy, negotiations, treaties and funding for legal systems, prisons and training of police officers. Technology has its place. Technology and the environment are not mutually exclusive events. Humans clearly can co-exist with the environment.

A future that works requires an understanding that history has surprised us. Karl Marx is required reading. The Communist idea of public ownership of the means of production has become reality. Today, the U.S. public owns the means of production in America. Over half of Americans now own some kind of interest in public companies either in their own retirement accounts or through their pension fund from their employer.[4] As shareholders in the means of production, you can vote and demand that corporate leaders redirect defense spending toward space and ocean exploration.

A future that works requires an understanding that the collapse of the fish stocks is happening. This is not hysteria. As Dr. Pauly and numerous scientists have made it crystal clear, this is real and it can be turned around. Close the high seas to commercial fishing. It sounds simple because it is. Most human created problems have solutions. If you don't like a dirty ocean and beaches, clean them. That is not complex.

A future that works requires us to expect the unexpected. The Iron Curtain came down, the Cold War ended, the Soviet Empire dissolved, the United States invaded Iraq, the American economy collapsed, fanatical Islam arose from the ashes of the Iraq disaster, the fish stocks are collapsing and now climate change threatens the entire planet. Most of these historic events were not foreseen.

Change is the only constant in human affairs. Three lifetimes ago, there were no electric toothbrushes, flush toilets, Toyotas, Tesla electric cars or televisions. There are good surprises, like cell phones, laptops and great information from history's largest library, the Internet. The entire social structure has changed in a mere 200 years from small agricultural communities to megacities and consumption and consumerism.

Obviously, the massive consumption that caused our environmental problems can be solved. Consume less. It is the small things done individually by a large number of people that have the greatest impact for change. Do simple things like buy lots of houseplants, grow your own vegetables, be prudent in your water use and have spayed and neutered pets. By surrounding yourself with life, you become more conscious of all of Gods' creation. Make your house an "urban jungle" that is compatible with nature. Recycle all of your newspapers, aluminum cans and plastic and glass bottles. Don't buy things, buy memories.

A future that works requires careful planning of what lifestyle we try to sell others. Our American lifestyle of consumerism does not bring happiness and is not attainable for the majority of the planet. It is clearly not compatible with the fragile ecosystem. If people in Asia, Africa and Latin America buy into the Madison Avenue materialism myth, we will sow the seeds of a nuclear, biological, chemical and environmental holocaust. You would need over four planets to enable the rest of the world to consume energy and materials like Americans.[5]

According to the Sierra Club's Dave Tilford, quoted in Scientific American:

> "The average American will drain as many resources as 35 natives of India and consume 53 times more goods and services than someone from China. Tilford cites a litany of

sobering statistics showing just how profligate Americans have been in using and abusing natural resources. For example, between 1900 and 1989 U.S. population tripled while its use of raw materials grew by a factor of 17. "With less than 5 percent of the world population, the U.S. uses one-third of the world's paper, a quarter of the world's oil, 23 percent of the coal, 27 percent of the aluminum, and 19 percent of the copper," he reports. "Our per capita use of energy, metals, minerals, forest products, fish, grains, meat, and even fresh water dwarfs that of people living in the developing world."

He adds that the U.S. ranks highest in most consumer categories by a considerable margin, even among industrial nations. To wit, American fossil fuel consumption is double that of the average resident of Great Britain and two-and-a-half times that of the average Japanese. Meanwhile, Americans account for only five percent of the world's population but create half of the globe's solid waste."[6]

Being the most gluttonous and obese society in human history comes with a price. We spend more money on "defense" than the next 20 nations combined. China, India, Pakistan and Indonesia have over 2.7 billion people. It is not realistic that they can all live in 2,000-square-foot homes and own two vehicles. The fossil fuel emission would be catastrophic. The efforts to control climate change would fail. Obviously, our conspicuous consumption lifestyle can't continue and cannot be adopted by the rest of the world as the model to measure human success. He who dies with the most toys still dies.

Possessions are like stones that weigh you down as you swim through the currents of life. The can be stolen, broken and require your time. With fewer material possessions, you will save the environment and free up your life. "Who needs it" will be the rallying cry of this century. Remember, "things" cannot love you. We have to be careful with the constant pursuit of possessions as often "things" are easier to acquire than to get rid of. Americans have so many "possessions" they build sheds next to garages to hold the consumer items that can't fit in the oversized homes. Thus, on weekends across America, there are yard sales where used goods are looking for buyers. There are swap meets where used items are sold and resold. We need to ask ourselves, do we own our things or do our things own us?

A future that works merely requires us to ask ourselves, "do I really need this thing and is it going to be occupying my shed, garage, or closet next year?" There is nothing wrong with consumption. What will work is buy what you need and use what you buy. Think of your lifestyle as "less is more". Moderation is the key to solving most of the planet's environmental problems.

As Mark Sagoff wrote in the Atlantic:

> "The world has the wealth and the resources to provide everyone the opportunity to live a decent life. We consume too much when market relationships displace the bonds of community, compassion, culture, and place. We consume too much when consumption becomes an end in itself and makes us lose affection and reverence for the natural world."[7]

Some problems are solving themselves. The population problem has not turned into the disaster predicted by the doom and gloom crowd of the 1960s. Education and economic development have put the brakes on the population explosion. As Swedish statistician Hans Rosling explained in the outstanding BBC program on "Over Populated," most families now have only two children.[8] As more people become educated, the population growth will eventually stabilize and is already reversing in the developing world. Many countries in Europe have negative population growth, as does Japan and Russia.[9]

A future that works requires an understanding that we humans are only a small part of creation; we are not creation. As we protect the two-legged ones, the four-legged ones, those who crawl in the sands, swim in the waters and fly in the skies, humans and the natural world will survive and life will spread to other worlds in other solar systems.

1 "Home." About ISO. Accessed July 26, 2015. http://www.iso.org/iso/home/about.htm.

2 2005, 12:01AM GMT 13 Feb, and Benjamin Joffe Walt. "'There Are No Laws. We Are in a Country Where No One Can Control Anyone Else'" The Telegraph. Accessed July 26, 2015. http://www.telegraph.co.uk/news/worldnews/africaandindianocean/somalia/1483442/There-are-no-laws.-We-are-in-a-country-where-no-one-can-control-anyone-else.html.

3 "Millions Lack Safe Water." Waterorg. Accessed July 26, 2015. http://water.org/water-crisis/water-facts/water/.

4 Domhoff, Glenn William. "Who Rules America: Pension Fund Capitalism." Who Rules America: Pension Fund Capitalism. Accessed July 26, 2015. http://www2.ucsc.edu/whorulesamerica/power/pension_fund_capitalism.html. Elert, Emily. "Daily Infographic: If Everyone Lived Like

An American, How Many Earths Would We Need?" Popular Science. October 19, 2012. Accessed July 26, 2015. http://www.popsci.com/environment/article/2012-10/daily-infographic-if-everyone-lived-american-how-many-earths-would-we-need.

5 "Use It and Lose It: The Outsize Effect of U.S. Consumption on the Environment." Scientific American Global RSS. September 14, 2012. Accessed July 26, 2015. http://www.scientificamerican.com/article/american-consumption-habits/.

6 Sagoff, Mark. "Do We Consume Too Much?" The Atlantic. May 31, 1997. Accessed July 26, 2015. http://www.theatlantic.com/magazine/archive/1997/06/do-we-consume-too-much/376877/.

7 Rosling, Hans, Professor. "OVERPOPULATED - BBC Documentary." YouTube. January 28, 2014. Accessed July 26, 2015. https://www.youtube.com/watch?v=-UbmG8gtBPM.

8 Ibid and Rosling, Hans, Professor. "The Best Stats You've Ever Seen." Hans Rosling:. 2006. Accessed July 26, 2015. http://www.ted.com/talks/hans_rosling_shows_the_best_stats_you_ve_ever_seen?language=en. see also, Rosenberg, Matt. "Countries With Negative Population Growth." Accessed July 26, 2015. http://geography.about.com/od/populationgeography/a/zero.htm.

Conclusion

"Kill the lawyers"
— WILLIAM SHAKESPEARE

The high seas will be closed off to commercial fishing. Humans will either volunteer or our great Earth Mother will close off the high seas for us. The fisheries will be slaughtered to extinction. The other choice is to do what we did with the buffaloes and whales. This is an environmental fight we can win. Humans saved the buffalo from certain extinction. Whales, mountain gorillas, elephants — there are battles out there we have either won or certainly made progress. There is no reason to lose this important historic battle to save the big fish. We just need to create a Global High Seas Marine Preserve for the benefit of the planet and future generations.

The legal framework created after World War II was ignored by the United States. Despite the great sacrifices of the brave Russian people, the Cold War was shoved down their throats. With over 20 million dead from a German holocaust and their industry in ruins, America initiated the Cold War to keep the economy from entering another Great Depression. The United States used nuclear weapons on a surrendering Japan. Whether we agree with this decision or not, the historical record is the Japanese were losing the war on every front. Both U235 and U239 weapons were used. After the Great Patriotic War, the U.S. threatened other nations with these weapons.

Obviously the Russians stole the designs and desperately built their own atomic bomb. So the United States upped the ante. The United States built the largest bomber force in human history that would fly right at the Russians 24 hours a day 365 days a year. The Russians responded by building the largest air defense system in human history.

Then the United States built the world's first hydrogen bomb — a monster weapon that was 1,000 times more powerful than the fission weapons used on a surrendering nation. The Russians in desperation followed.

The Russians have always had great engineers and mathematicians. They successfully launched the first satellite Sputnik into orbit on an economy much smaller than the United States. American policy planners could see intercontinental ballistic missiles with hydrogen bombs destroying the United States. The Russians never attacked. The United States responded to this "missile gap" with our intercontinental ballistic missile force. The Russians, desperate to not be slaughtered, followed with their ICBM force. They had experienced total destruction of their country. Their fear was real.

The United States was the first nation with a nuclear submarine. The Russians followed with their submarine fleet. Both countries made huge breakthroughs in jet fighters using captured German engineers and scientists to try to achieve air supremacy.

Both countries supported ruthless dictatorships all over the world. The United States invaded Vietnam and killed over 2 million people. When the United States overthrew the Marxist government of Afghanistan in Operation Cyclone in 1979, the Russians made the mistake of invading and killed over 1 million Afghanistan citizens. Clearly Afghanistan was better off before either superpower intervened in their internal affairs. Russian rule was better than the despotic disaster of the Taliban and the corrupt Karzai government that followed.

The United States was the first to land men on the moon. The Russians landed probes on Venus and achieved the same result on the moon using robots, not humans. During the brief lull in military competition, the two countries working with other nations have created a successful International Space Station. Russian Soyuz rockets deliver French, Japanese, American and other passengers to the space station.

Russia can lead the world away from an ecological abyss. They will have to do what they did during the Great Patriotic War, known in the West as World War II. Russia is going to have to lead humanity's journey to Mars. Other nations have made the successful journey to outer space and even a poor country like India has sent a probe to Mars. The journey to Mars is like the European race to the New World during the Age of Discovery. It will be explored and eventually colonized. But this is such a large endeavor the Russians cannot do it without help.

The reason the Russians should lead the way is they not only have a great tradition of space exploration, it will build trust again with the world. Invading the Ukraine was as irresponsible as was the West's overthrow of various Arab governments. Libya is worse off without Gaddaffi. Saddam Hussein kept the religious fanatics under control. Iraq is far worse off without the brutal dictatorship of Saddam Hussein. The United States helped Saddam come to power and overthrew him when he was no longer abiding by set rules expected of our dictators.

The conflicts in the Middle East will not burn out any time soon. Saudi Arabia has sponsored these Wahhabi religious schools of terrorism all over the Muslim world. Their demented view of reality has created conflicts all over the world. Until all of these teachers of fundamentalist Islam are arrested and their students are either stopped or killed, there will be no peace on this small planet. The Russians understand this reality.

Had it not been for the prudence of Mikhail Gorbachev, civilization would have ended in a nuclear war. The Reagan administration believed nuclear war was winnable and pushed the planet to the brink of disaster. When the Eastern block of the former Soviet Union wanted their freedom, Gorbachev could have ordered tanks into those countries but chose to let them decide their own fate with democracy. Gorbachev wanted peace but Reagan wanted American global rule. Peace would have to wait.

It is unfortunate that the Western powers decided to overthrow the corrupt government of the Ukraine in Russia's backyard. Russian President Vladimir Putin fell for the ploy and is now stuck in a war on his border. His better move would have been to leave it alone as the Ukraine is not a military threat to the Russian people. Invading was the worst mistake he could have made. Over 5,000 people have died and more continue to die each day. Obviously sanctions followed as well as a concerted effort to destabilize the Russian economy by driving down the price of oil — Russia's main source of revenue. Invading a country always comes with a price. This proved costly.

The Russians also have something the United States is currently lacking: great launch vehicles and an infrastructure that can ramp up for an increase in the space program. A space race to Mars is not a good idea. Mars needs to be developed as a human enterprise incorporating all nations.

The Russians led the world in defeating the Nazis. Four out of five German soldiers killed in World War II died fighting the Russians. The United States and Russia worked together and defeated the most powerful military machine in human history. Without Russian bravery and American industrial might it is quite possible the Axis powers would have won the Great Patriotic War. The Russians are a brave, smart people who want peace with the West. The live in a tough neighborhood; China is next door and Japan is on their doorstep. Russia has a large Muslim population that does not want to be under Russian control. They have been invaded numerous times and they take their defense matters seriously as for them it has been life and death.

But in order for Russia to lead, they will have to overcome their racism, homophobia and distrust of other nations.[1] Like the Japanese, Russia has a big problem with people's skin color. We are all God's children. We don't have to like each other, but to survive we better work together like we did in the Great Patriotic War. We have to treat each other with respect. Russian racism is repulsive and unacceptable. This is one of the real underlying reasons Communism never took off in other countries.

Russians can't stand non-white people. Their homophobia is repulsive and only hurts their own citizens. They need to get over it.

The United States needs to lead the world in making the high seas off-limits to commercial fishing. China can certainly help since they and the Japanese are a big part of the problem. China's investments in Africa require stability in that region. Many African nations bordering the oceans depend on the oceans for protein.

Without the major economic and military powers working together to explore the heavens and the oceans, the legal framework for peace will not be honored. Law after law and treaty after treaty have been initiated since World War II. These rules of behavior are just not followed because there is no enforcement since powerful nations do whatever they want. As Alan B. Sielen observed in his piece "How to Save the Oceans":

> "There is no shortage of international recommendations, action plans, and other prescriptions for restoring the oceans' health. The 1982 United Nations Convention on the Law of the Sea, the 1992 Rio Earth Summit, the 2002 Johannesburg World Summit on Sustainable Development, and the 2012 United Nations Conference on Sustainable Development (Rio+20) all put forward different ways to protect the oceans from pollution and overfishing, preserve biological diversity, and help developing countries build the scientific and institutional capacities to run effective conservation and management programs of their own. The calls for action have brought some victories,

such as international rules limiting what oil tankers discharge into the sea, a global ban on the disposal of nuclear waste into the ocean, and the creation of marine reserves, or protected areas of the ocean. But as much as these measures helped, they have not eliminated all the other threats to the seas."[2]

Without closing the high seas to commercial fishing, the fish stocks will be fished to extinction. This must not happen. As the buffalo were saved from certain extinction, we can win this environmental battle. It's not too late.

The Earth is a tiny spaceship traveling through space and time. It is a small planet circling a medium-size star at the edge of a large galaxy. We humans are just one species in a planet teeming with life. It is the center of the universe because we know only here there is life and plenty of it. We don't even know all of the different species of fish in the vast oceans. As we explore the oceans, we may discover new and even more exotic species in places we could not possibly imagine life existed. Earth is the center of the universe because it is our home. We are a mere 22 hours by jet from any major city on the planet. The planet is now one — all we need is a functioning legal system where we agree to play by the rules.

The United States must lead the world in upholding the law and working to expand it to the entire planet. Law is a sacred, fragile flower based upon the beliefs of the people. It can only grow if we pay attention to it and treat it with respect. Without law there is the collapse of the fish stocks, the extinction of numerous land species and barbarism. Law is the answer.

Humans are a very aggressive species. Finding proper outlets for that aggression is an important part of the social agenda of politicians who are truly interested in peace. The logical solution is to have people work and play together outside of the Earth's environment in outer space. The defense contractors are going to get the money regardless of the mission. Yes, it will be expensive. So is the world's current defense budget. Peace is worth it.

We can make this change happen. Join us in saving the oceans from certain disaster and in exploring the heavens. The organizations are out there. Find the one that fits your lifestyle. All of us working together will save the oceans and eventually land humans on Mars and later colonize it. This is our destiny.

Danny Quintana

---

1 Jackson, Patrick. "Living with Race Hate in Russia." BBC News. February 24, 2006. Accessed July 26, 2015. http://news.bbc.co.uk/2/hi/4737468.stm.

2 Sielen, Alan B. "Sea Change, How to save the Oceans." Foreign Affairs. April 16, 2014. https%3A%2F%2Fwww.foreignaffairs.com%2Farticles%2Funited-states%2F2014-04-16%2Fsea-change.

Index

C

M

N